BILLIONS UNDER PRESSURE

BILLIONS UNDER PRESSURE

THE ART AND SCIENCE OF CREATING, EXCHANGING AND PROTECTING VALUE

BY JARRETT PRESTON

CARRINGTON INTERNATIONAL PRESS

ISBN-13: 979-8-9882337-0-1- Paperback
979-8-9882337-1-8- Hardcover
979-8-9882337-2-5- eBook
LCCN: 2023907366

CARRINGTON
INTERNATIONAL PRESS

DEDICATION

This book is dedicated to Colonel Edward LaBounty, USMC (retired), a truly great man whom I met in his twilight years. You took the time to drive a young boy you hardly knew more than 2,000 miles from Seattle, Washington, to south Texas to begin my journey at the Marine Military Academy and went on to quietly fund my private scholarship without ever saying a word to me or anyone else. My life and my family's lives have been forever changed because of your generosity.

FOREWORD

I would like to begin this foreword by commending you as the reader and by recognizing the power of the knowledge you now hold in your hands! This book not only teaches a completely new perspective on value but also creates a defining moment for how high-net-worth individuals, family offices, businesses, and organizations, will create, manage, and protect their wealth into the future.

The author is uniquely positioned to take the reader on this journey after decades of consulting and advising some of the world's most successful individuals and families in their efforts to exchange and protect their most valuable assets! He has personally impacted my life and my outlook on the business of my family's valuable holdings since the very first day we met a number of years ago. His ability to concisely summarize the complexities of the subject matter will forever change your view, as it has my own.

For generations we have been led to believe that unique physical forms of value, such as real estate, fine art, private aircraft, yachts, and in my case, rare and precious gemstones and exquisite fine jewelry, can only be traded for one thing—fiat (money) and that our wealth can only be created, transferred, and protected by our ability to convert these physical assets into a paper currency that in the end we have discovered has far less value than what we have given in exchange. Well, no longer! The author has brought to light the truth that today we have new dangers and new solutions. He raises a global warning call to all of us who are concerned with building and managing significant asset portfolios for ourselves and our families that "diversification is no longer enough" and that without true "asset mobility" we no longer have the ability to protect and preserve wealth in an acceptable manner. He demonstrates how everyday political and economic events can be a killer of our lifelong efforts to create a financial legacy for our families, and shows that today, through technology advancement, we quite literally have near-instant access to value exchange for almost any type and any level of value with no geographical borders in terms of our personal economies.

He will walk you through how you, too, can create a plan to protect the value you currently hold while generating new pathways to build value into the future. As we begin to view and define value differently, we are awakened to the unlimited potential to establish, protect, and trade our own wealth in a calculated and secure manner. To date, these strategies and knowledge have been known and applied by only the very select—nation states, royalty, and the wealthiest private families in the world. Thanks to the author's diligent efforts, this knowledge is now available to the masses and thereby ushers in a new age of value exchange for all who can read, absorb, and take action on the information presented.

This book should be given to every entrepreneur, CEO, CFO, and chairman, so that they can be aware of the threats and the solutions that are present today! This is not a book for those who are afraid to look into the future (or into their current asset management and value transfer strategies and procedures)! This is a book for those who are courageous enough to ask, "Why are we not creating the value we have expected?" and "Why is our value seemingly stuck in one form or another while operating in a world that appears to move at lightning speed in all other areas?"

This book is not a light read for a holiday weekend to help you relax from the chaos of daily life.

This is a "breakdown of the reality of your perspective on value, a rediscovery of your courage, and redefining of your personal value trajectory" kind of read! I wish you great fortune, dear reader, as you go forward and learn of the wonders found in the history of value and critical new applications for balancing *billions* into the future.

Sincerely,
Rayaz A. Takat
Chief Executive Officer
TAKAT RARE AND UNIQUE JEWELS, est. 1955

TABLE OF CONTENTS

PART THREE: PROTECTING VALUE

INTRODUCTION

Imagine: you're enjoying a beautiful afternoon in your multimillion-dollar villa. The sun beats down on you, melting the ice in your cocktail. The children are in the pool; your spouse is sitting beside you, smiling, in her latest designer-swimwear acquisition. Your watch—which you've taken off and left on the table, in case you decide to go swimming—cost you nearly as much as that pool. The multiple collector cars in the garage? Even more. The private helicopter on speed dial? Even more than *that*. You have a private beach just down the hillside, where your 50-meter sailing yacht and 23-meter express cruiser are docked, and life is good.

Now consider the following: this home is beautiful and luxurious, yes, but it isn't perfect for you and your family any longer. You like it well enough, but for what you're paying every year to keep it, you should really love it . . . right? You are what you call "casually" on the market. You've "put out some feelers" for a buyer, but no one seems to want your beautiful property—at least, no one seems to want it for a fair price. While you do want to sell it, you want to sell at a price that makes sense for you, and you haven't had much luck even finding someone willing to make an offer allowing you to break even.

When you first thought of selling, you told your family to soak up the sun rays and really enjoy their last year here. Well, that was three years ago. You were not too worried, at the beginning. You were sure someone would buy it reasonably quickly for a fair price. After all, it is one of the five nicest properties on the island. While you haven't yet confided in your spouse, you're now worried that no matter what you do, you might not break even on what you've invested. She suggested redoing the guest house to make it more appealing, but pouring even more money into this asset doesn't sound like a great idea—in fact, while she might be right, doing so might end up just losing you even more money.

Above all, you're worried you might get stuck with this property. You're worried you'll never find a buyer, and the taxes and running costs (which are growing every year, on multiple assets) will drain you dry, taking years away from your retirement. You worry that your kids, getting older all the time, will inherit from you not a life of comfort, but a ball and chain in the shape of an impossible-to-sell vacation home.

You try to push it out of your mind and enjoy your weekend. It's *your* asset, and you deserve to enjoy it while you have it.

After all, a decent portion of your net worth is invested in this beautiful place, and you're determined not to spend what *really could be* your last summer here worried about finances.

Suddenly, from somewhere beyond the line of palm trees, you hear an explosion. It is painfully loud—it rattles your eardrums and the ice in your cocktail. The children freeze, look into the tropical jungle, then look back at you and your spouse, eyes wide. Your youngest starts crying immediately. Your oldest asks you what it was.

You rest the cocktail on the table and make your way over to the railing. You search the property line, the driveway, the palm trees, but see no movement. You knew things were getting bad with the local politics. You knew the local political tides were turning against the rich in this area of the country—which may have been part of the reason you were finding it difficult to make a sale—but . . . could it be that bad, that quickly?

No . . . that sort of thing doesn't happen to people like you.

Right?

It is quiet . . . then you hear men's voices. You hear the distant crackle of gunfire, and you see smoke.

Then you hear rioting.

Then more gunfire.

You gather the children inside, yell to your spouse to get everyone dressed and to find the dog while you frantically call for the helicopter. It won't be here for 10 minutes. *Ten minutes?!*

You glance around your home, at all the symbols of value you have obtained, all the things that contain within them evidence of your lifelong accomplishment. You have 10 minutes—an achingly long time to wait for safety, but a cripplingly short amount of time to save your assets. You have paintings here, jewelry, electronics—what do you save?

The cars are lost; you know that already. The art will not be recoverable, especially if you're right in guessing that the smoke is from a spreading fire. The yachts—very likely a loss if you can't reach the crew in time to instruct them to launch from the docks immediately. Maybe the crew has turned on you as well? The costs of these things flash before your eyes, spreadsheets and ticker tape dissipating into oblivion. You have some liquidity in the bank, of course, and you have some in the markets as well, but tens of millions of your net worth is *here*, in hard assets.

You thought you had time. You thought things were okay. You've waited for the right buyer, to maximize gains and minimize losses, but now you're not just about to lose several hundred thousand, but *the whole thing.*

You thought it would never happen to you.

But here you are, throwing on the first dry clothes you can find, grabbing a fistful of jewelry and your laptop, having to leave the rest behind. Forcing your sobbing toddler to choose just one stuffed animal. Corralling everyone up the spiral staircase onto the roof. The helicopter arrives just as the intruders climb over your back wall. Your children are crying; your spouse is crying. You lift off just as the fire catches on your back terrace.

Your work. Your investment. Your watch, which you forgot on the table by the pool. All gone, in a matter of moments—all turning to smoke before your eyes. Your family, traumatized and suddenly feeling significantly less secure than they were only minutes before, look to you for answers, for hope.

You have none.

This isn't fiction—this is real life. Situations just like this one have happened to people in the real world—in fact, they have happened to clients I've personally worked with. I've had a client forced to be airlifted when dangerous riots and attacks against the wealthy in his country reached his front gate. I've worked with families who have had to move from war-torn countries in a matter of days, leaving incredible wealth behind. Prior to engaging my firm and learning the critical strategies regarding value exchange and value preservation that we will cover in this book, these people were vulnerable targets, out in the open. Many times, their wealth was trapped in "unsellable" assets and even so-called "liquid" cash. Many times, all this went up in flames.

You may be at risk of something like this happening to you, right now. Maybe you know that, which is why you bought this book. Maybe you bought this book for another reason, and the last few pages were a bit of a wake-up call for you. Either way, it is my sincere hope that you are able to greatly benefit from the strategies I am about to share with you. These proven strategies are designed to ensure that you and your family can have much greater chances to avoid these dangers while securing your assets, even in today's turbulent global economy and into the uncertain future.

You do not have to wait in your current position until you risk losing everything. You do not have to watch helplessly as your value, trapped in assets you can't sell, disappears before your eyes, or your bank account, treading water, becomes inaccessible or useless to you and those you love.

It's a scary time in many ways—believe me, I know. But it's not hopeless. There is a way to create and manage value while curating safety and security in this dangerous world, and I will show you how.

Value-for-Value Exchange

My name is Jarrett Preston, and I work in the highly specialized field of value-for-value exchange, also known as asset trading. My days are spent working with clients who buy, sell, and trade unique assets such as fine art, yachts, mansions, castles, hotels, islands, aircraft and nearly everything else of rarity and high value. Those "priceless" assets often do have a price . . . much of which is hidden to the naked eye, and it's often even higher than you might expect. That 120-acre private island in Fiji might cost a small fortune to purchase, of course, but its *real* cost is not in cash; it is in time—specifically, the five or even 10 years it can take to sell to someone else. I am not exaggerating when I tell you that many people spend 20-plus years growing their wealth to the point where they can buy a private island—and then spend the next 10 to 20 years desperately trying to divest of it. If you are a person who has their own island or know someone who does, you're probably nodding your head right now. It's *that* common.

During my nearly two-and-a-half decades of experience in this field, I have curated and overseen multibillion-dollar trade portfolios of assets located across five continents. I have assisted clients in 40 countries seeking new avenues to facilitate high-value asset exchanges. I have worked with some of the world's most successful people, including private entrepreneurs, multigenerational-family offices, public figures, and even members of royal families, all of whom demanded the highest standards in professionalism and discretion. And I have delivered.

My team and I created the first global luxury-asset-exchange platform powered by blockchain technology, which is the first to market with an integrated solution. I can confidently say: I know this business of value front to back. What creates value, how it is perceived, who defines it, how pricing is associated (or not associated) with value, and why it can be so elusive to many at the most inopportune times. I am also keenly aware that the vast majority of the population does not realize how critical it is to understand the defining principles of value, for their own personal preservation and planning. Many of my high-net-worth clients have at times confused price with value and later learned the painful difference.

It may sound like a dream to own a megayacht, but anyone who has experienced it firsthand knows it is often anything but. Operating in this world of luxury often involves far more stress than any brochure would have you believe—but also potentially far more joy and freedom than you would have ever thought possible. It is this balance that I help my clients walk in daily.

To be clear—I'm certainly not here to dissuade you from making high-value acquisitions. In fact, I hope to encourage you to do so even more, but with a calculated approach and without having to worry about these downsides—potentially being unsafe, not being able to divest of the asset in your timing and on your terms, or having to worry about investing your hard-earned wealth into an asset that you may *never* be able to sell. I know how to move challenging assets, and I know how to transform value. And it is possible for you to do so as well in nearly any environment or situation, as long as you begin to prepare now. (You don't want to wait until the rebels are climbing your back wall, like the family in the introduction!)

Over my years working with clients in this field, I have learned, above all, the quintessential importance of value— and *not* just monetary value. I have learned the importance of gaining and keeping wealth sustainability and protecting the value you have accrued in every potential situation. I have learned that regardless of your current level of success, commitment is as critical to your management of value today as it was when you began your very first venture, and I have learned that diversification is no longer enough. In fact, mobility and security are of far more importance today than perhaps ever in history.

At the beginning of my journey, my clients were teaching me. Now, after decades in the field, I find that often I am honored to have the opportunity to teach my clients. It was, in fact, these clients that inspired me to share this knowledge with a greater range of people through a more universal process: this book. I wrote this book for individuals who have already achieved a significant measure of success, for those who own multimillion- and decamillion-dollar properties, rare fine art, luxury vehicles of all kinds, and other unique assets that require management and careful strategy. I wrote this book for those who desire to see their wealth grow, for their future and for future generations. I wrote this book to educate, to show every reader that despite what you may have been told by the market and perhaps even your mentors, you are *never* trapped in any single asset by any market condition. There is always a move forward to exchange tangible value. It is simply a matter of knowledge, preparation, relationships, and decisive action.

Despite what you may have been taught, you are able to skip the often long and painful steps of traditional sale and instead trade nearly any asset for another form of value that will meet your needs—without the need for cash getting in the way.

They say, "Cash is king."

I say, "Checkmate."

How to Read This Book

This book is set up in three sections:

    i.   Creating Value,

   ii.   Exchanging Value, and

  iii.   Protecting Value.

Within these sections are chapters that each will teach a critical lesson about value, with a focus on the importance of asset exchange as a strategy, and the most beneficial ways to exchange assets while maintaining discretion, security, and optimal value.

To illustrate my points, I have brought in stories from my own life, as well as stories from clients in similar situations as you may be in now. While the stories are true, I have changed all names and identifying details for the security and privacy of those involved. Discretion, as you are probably aware, is often of the utmost importance to clients of this caliber.

If you are a high-net-worth or ultra-high-net-worth individual or are on your way to becoming one, this book is for you. If you are reading this from your summer home in Ibiza, or from your boutique hotel and vineyard in Mendoza, which you've been thinking of selling (or perhaps even have been trying to sell), this book is for you!

Lastly, if you have accepted that the dangerous situation I laid out for you above is not out of a fantasy and *could* really happen to you, well, you are correct. And this book is for you.

Without further ado, let's begin our journey of value.

PART ONE:

CREATING VALUE

Chapter One

The Beginning of Value

"Price is what you pay. Value is what you get."
—Warren Buffett

The concept of asset trading is sometimes a bit strange to the newcomer, but even stranger is that perhaps unlike the modern person, our prehistoric ancestors were very familiar with the idea. When we picture prehistoric humans, we often picture small, isolated tribes living in caves—but this could not be further from the truth. Prehistoric humans were not isolated at all, but were very well connected to a level we would find extremely surprising, especially compared to the pop-culture view of early communities. In the 1960s, archaeologists recognized that through tracking the presence of obsidian, they were able to get a clear indicator of early humanity's trading networks, due to its rarity and how easy it is to identify its source. Obsidian is a naturally occurring volcanic glass prehistoric humans used to form knives, arrowheads, spears, and any number of highly valuable (at the time) tools. Obsidian, due to the way it is made, has various "tells" that scientists can use to determine where, exactly, it is from on Earth. By tracing how far obsidian tools have been found from the obsidian's respective volcanic origin(s), these scientists found no other explanation: there must have been a robust trading network among the Epipalaeolithic communities in the Fertile Crescent, even as early as 14,000 B.C.E.[1] That's about 10 thousand years before the first Egyptian pyramid was built. This was well before any gold standard, any universal standard currency—any currency at all! And yet, thousands of years before people thought to invent what we would call "money," there is clear evidence to support successful, long-spanning asset-for-asset trade.

Trade is in our blood.

The art of trade didn't stop there, of course. Asset trading, especially among long-distance partners, has never ceased playing a role in the story of human history. From the water-aided trade executed by the Phoenicians thousands of years B.C.E. to the exchanging of goods aided by caravans of camels thousands of years later—from the trades executed by the

---

[1]   Sherratt, Andrew. "The Obsidian Trade in the Near East, 14,000 to 6500 BC." ArchAtlas, 2005. https://www.archatlas.org/journal/asherratt/obsidianroutes/.

Vikings in the ninth century C.E. to the historic trade missions of Marco Polo centuries later, the concept of value-for-value trades executed over long distances helped to shape the ever-emerging world economy, as well as the wealth and prosperity of those directly involved in those creative exchanges.

Distant lands, back in the day, didn't have any use for foreign money. The local merchant wouldn't take coins from halfway around the world—what good were they? What they *did* have use for were assets. Things that had value beyond an arbitrary, mutually-agreed-upon designation. A one-dollar bill, after all, is made of the same material as a 100-dollar bill—we simply decided, collectively, that one is worth more than the other. However, a piece of gold transcends language and cultural barriers. An obsidian blade has inherent value that anyone can determine with a touch of the hand. Spices have value, fine tapestries have value, porcelain has value—and it is clear that this is true, no matter who you are. Assets have value, beyond the dollar sign often attached to them.

Larger networks like the Silk Road helped expand the world and shape it as it is today. Without the Silk Road, Europe would not have had access to life-changing Eastern inventions like paper, gunpowder, and—as its namesake implies—silk. Can you imagine England without tea? That's the world we would have lived in had it not been for asset trading.

The European discovery of the "new world" and the trade that it facilitated completely changed the established trade routes of the "old world" forever. Suddenly, new materials, valuables, and foods flooded the market—before this, Ireland didn't have potatoes, Italy didn't have tomatoes, and India didn't have spicy peppers! Now, these are ubiquitous with those area's cuisines, to the point that you'd have trouble visiting those places and avoiding those foods. This is just a microcosm of how impactful trade is; it is so impactful, it's impossible to imagine a modern world without it.

Trade doesn't just impact culture—it creates culture. It *is* culture.

Of course, the more modern forms of trade don't always look as simplistic nor as mutually beneficial as they used to. We have allowed fiat (cash) to interrupt these kinds of trades. But we don't need to be restricted to a single method of trade no matter how common it has become. We can learn lessons from our ancient ancestors who traded valuable obsidian for valuable animal furs or hearty seeds, which gave them surety about their future at that time. Asset-for-asset trading isn't just the past. It's very likely your future, too.

And it's my present.

Born Under Pressure

Like obsidian itself, I also began my journey under great pressure, and far away from where I ended up thriving in trade. In 1986, when I was 11 years old, my father abandoned my family, leaving my mother with no money, two children, and no formal career, education, or degree. He rocked our foundation— in less than 30 days, I lost my father, our childhood home, our car, and I had to drop out of my private school. While it wasn't as dramatic, it felt similar to the situation the family in the introduction found themselves in—suddenly, nearly all I had known and found comfort in was gone. All I took for granted, all that gave me confidence, all that I thought I'd have forever was swept out from under me.

This event was a monumental driver for me. I remember feeling that my father didn't value me as his son or as a person. As a result of this event, I developed a strong internal drive to show the world who I was, and what value I would become. Perhaps some of you can relate to this feeling and the personal resolve it can create.

I started working, as much as a child was legally able to. At our new home, a local low-cost apartment complex, I pulled weeds, swept walkways, and cleaned up as a maintenance assistant for the community. I remember helping to pay the electric bill one month at 11 or 12 years old with funds I had earned that month. My mother needed help, and intrinsically, I wanted to do all I could to be of value. I took my first "real job" at a pizza restaurant at age 13. I grew up pretty quickly, all told, and I knew the value of a dollar far better than my peers, but despite all this, I was missing that vital male influence that had disappeared with my father.

My grandfather was a U.S. Marine, so I suppose it came as no surprise that I wanted to follow in his footsteps. My freshman year of high school, I rode my bike to the local library (almost no one had a home computer in those days) and looked up the top military preparatory schools in the U.S. To my disappointment, I learned that tuition at leading military preparatory schools was nearly $25,000 a year all-in—which was nearly equal to my mother's current salary for an entire year! Obviously, they were not a realistic option, but I wrote them all letters anyway, hoping for a miracle. It was at one of these preparatory schools, I felt, that I would find my future. If only they would give me the opportunity.

Not long afterward, representatives of the Marine Military Academy came to an affluent area nearby to recruit new students. I begged my mother to go to the meeting, where I met the Assistant Commandant of the Academy. I wasn't doing especially well in school at that moment, but he saw something in me, something worth developing.

Shortly thereafter, I was offered a one-semester trial scholarship; I had to prove myself, and if I did, I was told they would take it from there. So, when I was 15 years old, a nearly-80-year-old friend of my mother's who was also a retired U.S. Marine Colonel, very generously offered to drive me thousands of miles from my home down near the Mexico border to Harlingen, Texas. I can still remember almost every detail about those three days on the road with him. From the roadside motels and buffet restaurants he seemed to love, to the 76-mile-per-hour cruising speed he demanded that we stay at no matter how close the car in front of us seemed to be—"don't touch the brake; they will move," he would repeatedly say. And he was right. He was a career Marine and a retired fighter pilot.

A serious individual indeed, who stood about six feet, three inches tall and to me looked like a bigger, tougher version of John Wayne. To say that those three days with him was a learning experience would certainly be an understatement. I had only just recently received my driver's permit, so I was not the most confident driver, but he insisted that I take the wheel almost the entire way to south Texas. Looking back now, I can see that he was pouring his wisdom, experience, and value into me every hour that went by as we drove along those desolate highways. Over 30 years later, I can still remember many of the statements he carefully placed into my young mind. At the time, I thought this person was simply a kind old man who offered to help a single mom and her son by driving me down to school. Later, I learned that he was so much more than this. I was nervous to be so far from home and everything I knew, but more than that, I was excited. As I stepped onto campus for the first time, I felt like I was stepping into my future.

This was a transformational environment for me, a new start to life. It was challenging, but I loved it, because I was able to demonstrate my value to people who treated me fairly and respected me as a person. I felt like they saw my hard work, and that my hard work was paying off. I "passed" my first semester trial with excellent marks, and the rest of my time at the Marine Military Academy was paid for by a privately funded scholarship. For years, I believed it was a scholarship earned only because of my hard work and academic excellence. I later learned that my "scholarship" was funded by the very same 80-year-old retired Marine who drove me all the way to the front gates to begin my journey at the Academy. He never told me. His only contact was to write me letters every several months encouraging me to work hard and give the greatest effort possible to succeed. I learned of this incredible gift that he had given me at his funeral just after I had graduated as one of the top performers of my class, receiving the Semper Fidelis Award. An honor bestowed upon only one cadet each year for excellence in all three areas of focus at the Academy: leadership, academics, and physical fitness.

Most people have a mentor, a teacher, a wise person ahead of them in their field they look to for guidance. Well, I like to say that the "Colonel" and the Academy *itself* were my mentors. I am the proud product of my time at the Marine Military Academy, Virginia Military Institute, and the United States Marine Corps. The lessons of relentless determination they taught me have stayed with me and forged my personality and career like magma forms obsidian. Thanks to them, I have overcome the example laid before me by my father. I was born under pressure, but instead of crumbling, I emerged as hardened obsidian.

Today, as a person, a businessman, a friend, a husband, and especially as a father, *my word* is my most valuable personal asset. At the Academy, one develops the habit of meaning what you say, and I always, to this day, say what I mean. This has helped me immensely as I carved my first path into the world of business.

First Steps

I felt the drive to build and demonstrate personal value through all this time, well into my 20s. I co-founded my first company in the real-estate-marketing sector in my early 20s, as I was asked to help with the venture and ended up becoming a partner. It was a surprising first step for me, but ended up being exactly what I needed to grow. We formed a regional marketing publication from nothing, and remarkably quickly after its founding, it was growing, with over 1,000 distribution locations and a wide readership.

I remember during our first months of business, we were short on credit and even shorter on cash. I was forced to negotiate with the commercial printers to print our magazine without advance payment, promising that I would cover them afterward and guaranteeing that we would be a very significant client for them. They balked, insisting we pay up front as all their clients did, insisting that they "were not a bank," but I was eventually able to convince them that my word was one of value. They printed the issue, we paid them, and it was a successful relationship for all parties.

They had faith in me, because of the strength of my word. This was not the last time something like this happened. There are benefits to always saying what you mean and meaning what you say, not the least of which is the foundation of trust.

Publishing was never in my plans; the opportunity simply appeared, and I seized it. Due to this, I was not exactly passionate about keeping this company in my hands. This company was subsequently sold to a leading franchise of a global real estate company less than one year after its founding. That experience and accelerated success opened doors for me to become a highly-sought-after business development coach, sales trainer, and multidimensional consultant. I was offered opportunities to consult nationally in the real estate industry, specifically business development and business coaching. I spent three years after exiting the first business honing my skills and building a larger national and international network.

It was during this time that I discovered the potential of value-for-value exchange and the many benefits it could provide for individuals, families, and companies owning substantial physical assets worldwide.

Forging Obsidian

The aha moment about assets occurred very early on in my career. In fact, it occurred as I almost accidentally completed an asset exchange of undeveloped land assets for a boat.

I was looking to purchase a boat—as any very young man who recently exited their first company would think was a good idea. Real estate? Savings? Something for my future? No way—I wanted a boat! (Some of you are laughing at that—because you may have done something similar, too!) So I was negotiating with the broker for the acquisition, and in that process he learned I had a business that, because of the name of it, he assumed was in real estate holdings. He didn't realize it was a marketing media publication—he just knew the name of the company, and that I was in the metro Atlanta area, which, at the time, was really booming. The market was *on fire* there; there were some very strong returns on real estate. He asked if I might have any real estate that I would want to trade for this boat instead of purchasing it with cash.

I thought to myself, W*ell, that's quite interesting.* Trading property for a boat, without cash getting involved at all? I'd heard of trading baseball cards for packs of gum, and I myself used to make small trades between my fellow Marines when out in the field for training exercises, but I'd never heard of trade at this level of value. Cash was king, and at the time, for me, cash was the only king in the kingdom I thought we were all living in. Turns out, I couldn't have been further from the truth.

Amazingly, while I didn't own a real estate company at that time, he wasn't too far off target. I didn't have a real estate company, but I did actually have two pieces of real estate that I had previously acquired in trade for marketing/consulting services. I had figured trading land with a developer for services was one thing, being a complimentary exchange of sorts, but land for a boat? That felt like a whole different opportunity entirely. I didn't really want the real estate, so I told the man that I was in possession of two undeveloped home lots that were worth approximately the same value as the boat. We wound up agreeing to exchange that very real estate for the boat I wanted to buy from him.

I walked away from that transaction completely blown away by how easy and effective trade could be. It was that aha moment when I remember thinking, *How interesting. I'm not writing a check or spending cash for this boat. I'm simply trading something that I acquired in the past, that I no longer need, for something that I prefer to own.* Of course, I could have sold the land assets and used that money to buy the boat, but that could have taken weeks, months, or maybe longer. And who knows? Maybe the boat would no longer be available, or perhaps the market would take a dip, causing the properties to lose market value, not yielding enough to buy the boat in the long run. Instead, through the art of trade, I had what I wanted, he had what he wanted, and we were both happily down the road.

It was truly amazing how straightforward it was. So simple and effective.

After the exchange, I thought about the speed and seamlessness of what had just occurred, and the light bulb went on. Might there be many other people out there who own significant assets they no longer desire to own, who might be willing to trade—or, in fact, be *excited* about trading—those assets for other forms of value that better suit their future plans? Might others want to skip the long, arduous process of a traditional sale—going in and out of cash and losing valuable time all the while? I began to inquire around and discuss this idea with property owners and other asset owners, and realized quickly that there was a significant sector of the market that demands full value for their assets, but does not necessarily require fiat (cash) for such value.

The founding of my first asset trading company started very humbly with an idea and many questions. Within 30 to 40 days, I found myself with 50-plus "leads," parties who owned beautiful, valuable assets who were willing to trade and—it seemed—even pay me to assist them in exchanging those assets for something else of comparable value, eschewing cash in the process. In the beginning, the list was simply pieces of paper with the details of a property or catamaran sailboat, or car collection, as well as a list of other assets the owner might consider trading theirs for. Before I knew it, I was on the phone working to build relationships and present potential matches with some of the most successful people on the planet.

I could see, very quickly, that my idea had merit. Within the first several weeks, I was able to identify two "clients" who seemed to be a match for each other. Keep in mind: at this point, I had no formal processes, no team, no website, no *company,* even, and no trail to follow. Again, I found myself mentorless, as I could find no other company doing such transactions to model my work after. In the beginning, I had only a spark of an idea and the commitment to see it through to reality. Also, of course, I had my military training and mindset, which gave me the confidence, follow-through, and integrity I needed to make it work, despite my lack of experience.

Less than six weeks in, I facilitated my first client trade. They asked me what they owed me for the service. I honestly had no idea what to charge, but I believed in the value I was able to provide and quoted a price that was perhaps less than they expected but more than enough to make me excited to repeat the process again. I was on cloud nine when the first deal was done and they wired me my consulting fee. I stared at the numbers in my bank account, and thought, *Wow—and I can do this every single month!* (Well . . . I was wrong about that!)

After taking time to set up a company properly, build a web portal, and do everything else I needed to do, I obtained contract advice and began to build our first formal database. I was excited, ready to hit the ground running, ready to help the rich and famous make the perfect trade, ready for my bank account to double and triple in a matter of weeks. Then . . . nothing happened.

Nothing happened for *almost six months!*

I worried, at times, that that first lucky transaction I had pulled off might have been a one-time event. A fluke. Regardless, each day I continued to build my network and database of potential traders and assets, running on faith as my bank account slowly depleted.

Finally, after nearly seven months with no more success and no income, I met another client who engaged with me as seriously as the first one had. I tried not to get overly optimistic, but still poured my heart into working with them and trying to secure a suitable trade partner. Then, I found their match: a party who was also fully ready to transact under the right parameters. There was a familiar momentum to the discussions—I began to realize a pattern of prospecting, qualification, relationship building, and finally real business engagement. Just a few days after meeting these new clients, I found myself at one of the most beautiful mansions I had ever seen—but I wasn't there as a mere guest or visitor. I was there as an asset trading consultant.

I still remember when one of them introduced me to his attorney using this title. This is Jarrett Preston, my *asset trading consultant.* I remember hearing those words and feeling a sense of pride, accomplishment, and empowerment. Nine days later, I sat with both clients as they closed their transaction and thanked me for my efforts to assist them. This was the second trade I had facilitated for clients, and this time the fee was *much* larger than the first one. I was able to breathe easy for the first time in months as I saw that concept had become reality. It was official: I was, indeed, an asset trader, an asset trading consultant. And I was now certain that this was not a fluke. In fact, it was the beginning of an extraordinary journey.

Valuable Trades, Invaluable Lessons

While these first couple trades were a major benchmark for the development of the business and my personal trading confidence, successes like these were far less valuable and less frequent than were the many failed transactions I attempted to facilitate along the way—especially early in my career. Such as the time I flew to a country thousands of miles from home to meet a new client who had signed a memorandum of understanding to trade his 35-meter sailing yacht … who then *never* showed up. I remember being so frustrated that I could find myself in such a position where I had spent days of time and thousands of dollars out of pocket to arrive at nothing! But it was situations like these that helped to build the qualifying processes my company and I personally have operated with now for decades, and still do today. Those experiences, while incredibly frustrating at the time, were invaluable to my growing ability to successfully model what will and will not lead to success in this industry for my clients.

That was not only a lesson to me about unqualified/uncommitted transaction partners. In this case, it was also a lesson learned by the client. Many months later, the client called me back and wanted to meet again to begin working together, but I had learned my lesson and was not about to repeat the process. I thanked him for thinking of me but told him I would not be meeting him, and though I was kind to him, I reminded him that he had missed our meeting in the Caribbean with no call and no courtesy and that I wouldn't be taking that path again. My word is good, and I expect my clients' word to be good, as well. In my experience, that kind of trust is the only way to make successful trades of significance. Four years later, I ran into him at a yacht show in Fort Lauderdale, Florida. He was *still* trying to sell the same vessel, and at a substantially lower value than we had been discussing, of course. At that rate, there was no way he wouldn't be losing massive value on that transaction. I would have been able to do so much better for him. I remember smiling inside, just a little.

Beyond the skills of the trade, this process of starting from nothing taught me to never fear mistakes. When you are just starting out, you will make mistakes. You're still learning, you're new to the process, so it's bound to happen. Beyond mistakes, you will also encounter personal struggles that are not your fault. However, I don't believe we should allow ourselves to be tied to our mistakes and setbacks—no matter how costly those mistakes may be.

Mistakes will happen, but in the end *failure* cannot be an option. My early life training at the Academy and in the U.S. Marine Corps taught me that your level of commitment will drive you through your challenges and into your success, no matter the venture. If you have already reached a significant measure of success, you know this to be true already.

When you were building your value initially, you may not have had the wisdom or experience needed to properly diversify or structure your assets in a beneficial manner. Because of this, at times, your value building may have stalled—or even been substantially reduced due to the depreciated value of a major personal or business asset. Perhaps you have arrived in that situation where you feel trapped in an asset, and you may feel like you are going to lose no matter what. I have been there.

I'm here to tell you that all is not lost when such moments arrive. There are solutions to nearly every such situation—even yours, no matter where the asset is or what the challenge might be. Let's go through a few common situations now, so I can prove this to you.

Let's say you have an asset you no longer want to own, or now perhaps even wish you had never acquired it. What do you do with a mistaken purchase?

If you find yourself in the position of owning an asset that has not turned out to be everything you hoped for, or no longer meets your needs for any reason, the first step is to evaluate what you have and what practical options exist to exit the asset. When I say evaluate what you have, I am referring to taking the time to clearly establish the asset's current market value, or to determine if there is even a market for this asset at all in current conditions. Understanding the viability of a traditional sale, as well as any other options you have to monetize the holding, is a critical first step. Depending on the type of asset, you may have options to sell it privately or publicly. Alternatively, you might be able to rent it, or in some cases even leverage the asset to generate immediate liquidity, giving you more time to design and implement a permanent solution—though leveraging is a worst-case option in most scenarios. Or, as we often find is the best strategy for debt-free assets, you may be able to simply trade it for a preferred asset class that better meets your needs.

What if the market conditions for your asset seem to be stagnant, indicating you have waited "too long" or perhaps missed the market completely, leaving no viable options to sell the asset traditionally, nor any of the other primary avenues mentioned above? In this case, I would advise you to take three steps right away:

1. Take immediate action. Do not, under any circumstance, simply sit and wait.

2. Contact no less than three unbiased, highly regarded professionals who know the market and know the asset class you are dealing with and ask them to evaluate the options and give you a realistic opinion of the strategy and time frame to divest of the asset. Ask them what they would do if it were their own asset/situation. You might be surprised by their answer. If they are a top performer in their field, they will have insight you have not thought of and likely will suggest strategies you have not considered. Quality advisors in this space are invaluable, no matter how experienced you may or may not be. Of course, each asset class and geographic location requires very unique knowledge to create an effective plan.

3. Contact our company for a confidential discussion and evaluation of the asset and, more importantly, the potential options available to complete a value-for-value exchange to move you out of the asset immediately and into a new holding that better meets your needs now and/or provides more options to you for the future.

What can you do when acquiring new assets in the future to prevent you from making the same mistakes again? Well, may I humbly suggest that you consider contacting us before you make the purchase? My team and I have worked alongside clients facilitating high-value transactions for nearly every type of asset imaginable. From private aircraft and superyachts to iconic estates, private islands, land assets, rare fine art, one-of-a-kind fine jewels and mineral reserves, if it is rare and/or of significant value, we *can* assist you with the proper planning prior to making an acquisition and often can assist you in designing a strategy that will allow you to keep all or most of your cash liquidity and instead utilize currently dormant assets to acquire your next valuable holding—but I'm getting a little ahead of myself. We have a lot more to cover first.

In Summary

We all start from the bottom—as raw material, like the magma under the crust of the Earth, which eventually grows above the surface to create obsidian. We have each had *different* trials and tribulations, but none of us have made it to where we are now without tremendous pressure and challenges along the way. This forging process has brought us to where we are today—hopefully now in a position to begin thinking about our asset strategy in new ways and specifically how value-for-value exchange can help us in the modern era. I can confidently commit to helping you along this important journey. I hope you equally commit to taking the plunge with me.

We all make mistakes, especially at the beginning of our journey of building value—typically due to lack of experience or knowledge. Even humanity made mistakes when they first invented asset trading with obsidian stone—I'm certain none of them thought of creating insurance products to mitigate their risk, and none considered facilitating transactions via blockchain for a transparent and more secure transaction! These were obviously not options then so were never able to be considered at all in those early days—but this is precisely my point. The only thing consistent about value creation, preservation, and trade over the last several centuries is change itself. Value is fickle, and value is personal, and because of this, it can be very illusive. This is especially so in the modern era we operate in today where change is happening across every part of our lives at record pace.

The key is not to get held up by our mistakes, but to learn from them and look brightly toward our future. The key is to stay committed to finding solutions even in the midst of market turmoil and constant change. The key is determination and commitment. The measurable difference between someone who makes a mistake and gives up and a person who makes a mistake and keeps going is simply *commitment*. Commitment is very different from involvement. While this is not a personal development book by any means, you will hear this concept coming through several times in the pages ahead: commitment is not involvement. Let it really sink in. Understanding this fact can make all the difference when on a journey to create, manage, and protect value.

But what is the meaningful difference between the two, and how does this possibly apply to your asset management?—I can almost hear you asking. So, without further ado, let's dive into the next step: the meaning of commitment and the importance of it to your business, to your asset portfolio value, and your life.

Chapter Two:

Establishing Leverage Through Commitment

"Commitment is what transforms a promise into reality."
—Abraham Lincoln

Allow me to get straight to the point. I want you to imagine an amount of income that would be incredibly difficult for you to earn in one year. I am suggesting a number that is twice, triple, or—even better—*10 times* your current average annual income, whatever that may be. Do you have the number in mind? Okay, good.

Let me ask you a very direct question: could you earn that amount of income in a single year if you had to? Ten times your average annual income. Be truthful. Take a moment and ponder the question and the difficulty of such a task. Odds are, your answer is "no." You've tried, of course—who doesn't try to earn as much as possible? But there are always limitations to the amount of income one seems to be able to earn. Red tape you can't cut through. Expensive emergencies that cut into your overhead. Market failures or global pandemics you couldn't predict or couldn't control, and, barring that, there are holidays to take, time off to enjoy, and employees that you delegate some of that responsibility—and potential earnings—to.

Okay, so we've agreed that you can't earn that amount of money in one year. That's fine. There's no realistic way. All right.

Now I want you to visualize something very different: the face of the one person you love most in this world. It can be more than one person as well. Perhaps it's the two or three people you love most in this world—maybe your spouse, your significant other, your children, or a sibling or parent. Take a moment to clearly visualize their face(s) in your mind—the person or people you love more than anyone or anything else. (This can't be yourself, by the way! I know some of us have healthy egos, so I thought I should mention that.) Can you see the face(s) clearly in your mind? Their eyes, their smile? Can you hear the sound of their laughter? Maybe you're smiling, just thinking about them. Good. Now let us remember that commitment has often been described as the trait of sincere and steadfast fixity of purpose binding oneself intellectually and emotionally to a given task. Let's embrace this for a moment as I ask you to contemplate the next scenario and question.

Now imagine for a moment that, if next year you *don't* earn the income you decided on above (10 times your current income), the income that you claim is impossible to achieve next year, that this person/these people will no longer be alive in 365 days.

For whatever reason, if you don't reach that income benchmark with cleared funds in your account, their breath will stop and they will no longer be alive. No doubt for many we are talking about your spouse, your children—or another very close loved one, the person or people you love most in the world.

Let me ask you the question again in a different way. Could you find a way to earn that level of "impossible" income in one year now? . . . To save their life?

I think I know the answer for most of you: yes, you could, and yes, you would! You see, you would no longer do what is popular or traditional, you would no longer have a normal schedule or action plan, nor would you take multiple vacations or days off or work halfway focused throughout the week. You would do whatever it took, spending all the time and resources you have to earn what is necessary to save their life. You see, you wouldn't just be involved with your business strategy any longer—you would be *committed to it! Committed* to making the largest possible successes you could manage, as you put absolutely 100 percent of your heart and soul into every moment in order to beat the clock and save your loved one(s). And you would do it, too. I know you would, because I would. Anyone of high value would. There is no limit to the level of effort and focus we would operate with in such a situation.

This example demonstrates the very simple but powerful difference between being *involved* and being *committed*. It is quite extraordinary what we can do when we truly become committed. Keep this in mind, as the power of this principle of commitment will come up multiple times throughout our journey together, and throughout your journey of managing and creating value in your own life. Understanding this and anchoring to this principle will be especially important when markets seemingly turn suddenly against you, leaving little margin for error with regard to personal asset management decisions.

True Commitment

At the Marine Military Academy, I began to learn what true commitment really meant. In a military environment, you simply don't say you're going to do something you don't do, and you can't say you aren't going to do something you do end up doing. If you are not true to your word in the military, someone will likely lose their life. For that reason, if your squad member asks you to cover them, *you cover them.* Commitment very quickly became a matter of life or death for me.

In the same way, there are also life-or-death moments for businesses and high-value transactions, tense moments when, if a deal falls through or a major step doesn't occur, the business will die and dreams will shatter. Earlier I shared details with you about a moment when this happened for me—when the printers didn't want to print our magazine because we couldn't pay them in advance. If they didn't print our issue, the company would not have any product to sell. We would have been completely over and done with—and I simply couldn't let that happen. I couldn't have the first business mark on my record be black with failure. I was committed. So, as a young and inexperienced entrepreneur, I bargained with men double and triple my age and experience to get done what needed to get done. I succeeded, and they printed the magazine for us, and they got paid, as did I. By that action, not only did I save the business, but likely saved my future career as well—and secured a nice *future* paycheck for my "value exchange partner," which they quickly realized as we became very good customers.

This only happened because I was committed to the outcome and intrinsically understood the principle of value-for-value exchange!

If I wasn't committed—if I was merely involved in that moment—I might have simply shrugged my shoulders and left when they clearly said "no." I probably wouldn't have been able to find another printer, and I probably would have been completely out of luck. I never would have printed that issue of the magazine, or received that incredible leg up that led to many consulting opportunities and the formation of my first asset trading firm and, eventually, a global venture: Idoneus, where I serve as CEO today.

Whether on the battlefield, in the business arena, or in the midst of a personal moment of crisis, I will place my bet on the most committed person every time. It's not wealth, or experience, or education that will yield the greatest returns in these moments. Ninety-nine percent of the time success goes to the most committed. This is a principle that I have seen save and cost individuals many millions of dollars—depending on their level of awareness and application at a key moment in their life.

I have made a commitment to practice this principle even if many others do not. Many people we meet will merely be involved and will pass through our lives with little impact. My father clearly wasn't committed to us, and he didn't deliver on his promises. But I have discovered the power of commitment and have made it a matter of personal practice to commit and deliver, in every way possible, to every client and for every promise. Even though I personally have been through divorce and all the difficulties that come with it, my children are experiencing the exact opposite of what my father allowed us to experience. They know if I say something, I mean it. If I say we're leaving at five o'clock, we're leaving at five o'clock *on the dot.* You can set your watch to my commitments! If I say we're going to Paris this summer, they know they can get excited and start practicing their French, because *nothing* that is within my power or influence is going to make me cancel that trip. I endeavor to live a life fully committed to every word, every action, and every business connection I make. I can confidently encourage you to do the same. It is not a guarantee of a life without failures and perfect success, but it will greatly stack the odds in your favor 99 percent of the time.

I once received a lead: the founder of a major, global company was in the market for a private island. The price was no object to this person—what really mattered was the wind.

Quite seriously. The *wind* was where the value was to be found for this transaction.

This was because this person had a passion for windsurfing, so the island had to have the right kind of wind at the right time of year for optimal windsurfing. Otherwise, the island wouldn't be valuable to this person. After all, what's the point of owning a private island if you can't even use it for your favorite activity?

It might sound superfluous, but if you're in the market, you know it's anything but. Many people have jumped into enticing purchases like islands and yachts without thinking them through, and ended up having to go through the arduous task of selling (or trading) them later, when they discovered they didn't fit their needs. It can happen to the best of us, and managing these mistakes for others has made up a lot of my career—but I digress. We'll discuss more about that later.

This person was very intelligent and even more demanding in terms of detailed criteria, and was trying to get it perfect from the start, so they wouldn't have to go through a very long and difficult sales process later. I can respect that, and I knew my team and I could find the right property for the potential client and their family—and all their windsurfing needs.

Well, my team and I spent many weeks researching on- and off-market properties and learning about the different types of wind each island had. I learned more about wind currents than I'd care to admit. In the end, we were able to present a few truly inspiring options, and we deeply impressed this potential client with our attention to detail, because it was obvious we went the extra mile for them before we even requested a contract for services.

This illustrates another of my core principles, which is: you must give value before you request to receive value. This is also why for my entire career we have charged zero fees up front: because I believe it is vital that we prove our value before asking any client to give us value in exchange. This extends even to today with Idoneus, where we have been able in many cases to remove all costs for sellers and buyers who transact through the platform.

Back to the wind—the client was impressed, but unfortunately, even after all that work, we didn't get the trade! Well, that wasn't so unusual. In fact, back then, we didn't get 90-plus percent of the deals we did this kind of extensive research for, but we put our whole hearts into the research anyway. *That* is showing our value to the client. *That* is proving that *we* value *them,* and that we understand what *they* value. *That* is providing evidence of commitment.

Despite the fact that historically we didn't close 90-plus percent of the contracts we started working on, I hold true to the belief that failure is not an option. How can that be? Because these are not *failures*, necessarily, but *incompletions.* Even so, we don't call it a 90 percent incompletion rate; we might call it a 10 percent success rate! Which in our business, prior to new technologies coming forth to revolutionize the industry, was not bad at all!

I sometimes like to put it in terms of American football. We are not the wide receiver, running flashy routes for long first downs or touchdowns on every possession—rather, we're the running back taking the ball on nearly every play right down the center of the field through the most difficult traffic imaginable. We're watching every play, studying every move along the line, ready for that one moment, that one brief pause in the defense that opens up a hole that we can sprint through. We might not see this opportunity for half of the entire game, but when we finally get our moment, you better believe we'll be in position to score and have the whole audience cheering and on their feet. And we only get this opportunity if we are 100 percent focused, 100 percent of the time. Eyes open, ready for our time to shine.

Anyone who has been in business as long as I have would agree that it seems few people are truly dedicated, truly committed, and true to their word today. It is almost a lost art to be a man or woman of your word. I have found this to be the difference-maker in my business and in my life, as well as the lives of my most successful clients. It takes more than just "showing up" and "being present," shaking hands, and signing contracts—you have to put your back into it and actually deliver what you promised to deliver. This is not a job where you clock out at 5 p.m. and don't think about your work again until 9 a.m. the next day. To really succeed here, you have to put your heart into it. You have to put your *all* into it, as if your loved ones' futures were on the line.

I see this quality in many of my clients, which is probably why they are where they are today: typically, in a position of great enough wealth and success to be trading debt-free, high-value assets that most can only dream of. Qualities like this are a rare find, and they cause one to stand out when in a crowd of people (even a crowd of other successful people) who are merely "involved." You've probably ended up in a conversation with someone who is merely "involved" with their business—a business they've inherited, or a business they are seemingly leeching off of as it nosedives into an avoidable crash. The kind of person who, despite having a flashy title like "managing director," doesn't seem to have really worked a day in their life. These are the kinds of people who never have circles under their eyes from a long night on a project, or who skip board meetings because some dime-a-dozen entertainer is in town. These are the kinds of people you hardly want to share the check with, never mind a high-value asset exchange.

Despite the comparably smaller field we're working with today, I am able to find committed individuals simply by searching for those who exude honesty and genuineness. People who don't honor their word are always suspicious of other people not honoring their word—therefore, we must keep an eye out for those who are projecting their own untrustworthiness onto others. This is especially important when identifying professionals to assist us or even trade/business partners. You never want to trade with the guy who makes it clear over and over that he thinks you're ripping him off; odds are, well, *he's* probably ripping *you* off.

The power of commitment is applicable for everything—for business, for relationships, for goal setting, and even asset management strategy—in this turbulent world we now live in. Those who commit to providing value above all else experience results that the involved can only dream about.

Patience in Commitment

I am reminded of a client I met well over a decade ago. He was introduced by one of my bright, young team members in business development at the time. This client had real potential. He was an owner of more than $50 million in extraordinary assets that he no longer wanted to own, he seemed to have high integrity, he was open to flexible exchange options, and he was basically the perfect asset trading client. I remember trying to convince the team member who introduced him to our firm that we needed to fly to see this new client in person as soon as possible.

The team member told me, "I can't fly thousands of miles and take three days of time to go meet this person when I don't even have a deal lined up yet."

I reminded him that we invest our value first in order to potentially receive value in return in the future. The greatest way to do this, of course, is to build relationships and show our clients that we are fully committed to the mission. In the end, I could not convince him to go. I believe that because of that team member's hesitance, we almost missed out on one of our absolute best clients.

This client became one of the most important clients of my entire career, and not because of his personal assets, but much more so because of the many relationships he has brought to our company through his extended network and high-value connections. It took about a year to develop any solid business with him after that initial introduction, but since then, this client brought perhaps more value to me and our partner companies than any other single person.

Unfortunately, the team member who introduced this client was merely involved and not committed. He left our company just prior to the first significant business being completed and never tasted the benefits of staying patient in commitment. This was a very costly mistake on his part.

The Test of True Commitment

Something a lot of people in my field have a hard time learning is that a client not agreeing to work with you is not, necessarily, someone who isn't "committed" to their outcome—they are simply not committed to working with *you*, which you can't take personally. I've always been especially talented at letting criticism roll off my shoulders, but as I'm sure you're aware, this skill does not come to most so easily.

Let's take the business leader who wanted an island for windsurfing. If you remember, that client didn't end up transacting with our company. However, they did—last I heard—manage to find the perfect, wind-filled island for themselves, through another source. I wouldn't call this person "not committed." They got what they wanted, and did what was best for themselves. If anything, they were very committed! (By the way, we didn't come out of this empty handed; in that process, while we didn't close that specific transaction, we did build a valuable relationship with the exclusive asset manager for one of the wealthiest individuals on Earth—not a bad ROI for our commitment to delivering value before receiving any in return!)

No—a person who is not committed is not synonymous with a person who opts not to work with you. I've actually already told you the story of a client who didn't commit: the client who stood me up, after I had flown to another country to meet him. After that, I didn't want to work with him—and he must have done a similar thing to others in the space, because no one else seemed to want to work with him, either. In the end, he was stuck trying to sell his yacht on his own, at a much greater loss than he would have if he had just committed from the beginning instead of letting other things take priority. If he had committed to me and my company, I am 100 percent certain I could have secured him a much more valuable exit trade than he achieved—we might have even gained value in other ways by the end of our collaboration, and perhaps might have developed a great working relationship. He might have forged great relationships or valuable business associates from within my client network, solving problems and expanding his other ventures like so many of my clients have done. He missed out on tremendous value, but he didn't have to, and neither do you.

When venturing into a value exchange of any kind, you must be committed, and you must demonstrate your commitment to all parties involved. I'm looking out for it, and the best of the best in my field are all looking out for it, too. If you want to get ahead of the game, you'll start looking for it in your trading partners, as well (and everywhere else in your life), if you don't look for it already.

Check your commitment level. How sure are you about the outcome you intend to achieve? Are you certain that your current path is taking you to the destination you say you're headed to?

If your consistent daily actions are not aligned with your commitment, there's no two ways around it: you *will*, 100 percent, find yourself stalling or lacking progress in the areas you know are critical to secure yourself and your family. I cannot stress this enough. Average commitment will never lead to extraordinary outcomes. A typical year of involvement will never get that "10 times your income" we discussed in the example at the top of this chapter.

Let me encourage you to tie commitment to everything you do and every decision you make in terms of your asset management. Involvement is not enough to protect your family's legacy in this day and age. Involvement will not secure your future in the manner your family deserves. After working with thousands of people from all walks of life and nearly every continent, I can confidently say that it has been the most committed people who have reached the highest levels of success in this area. Commitment will outperform pedigree, it will outperform intellect, it will outperform education, it will even outperform market conditions (this is very key for you) if you are operating in the world of high-value asset holdings. In our earlier exercise, you learned that it is possible to increase your income by 10 times with a single committed decision. That level of leverage on yourself will not only impact your life financially in terms of asset management and the strategies we are discussing here, but in every critical area of your life. It is that important.

Let me encourage you to think about where else you might need to adjust your standard of commitment. Is it your goals that need clarity and commitment? Perhaps it's a business, or it may be a relationship? Maybe you already have the level of commitment needed and now you need to consider situations you should walk away from? Knowing when to walk away is as important as knowing when to fight for completion. Remember, not completing is not the same as failing. At times, we need to walk away from transactions, assets, or relationships that are not serving us and moving us toward our goals. Accepting the need for change is not to be confused with a lack of commitment. One of the most powerful demonstrations of commitment is seen in one's ability to make hard decisions and re-prioritize to move toward your success.

But at the end of the day, when it comes to transactional commitment . . . needing to be committed is not really a requirement for all. Does that surprise you, after such a focus on commitment? It might, but the truth is, my clients don't have to be committed. We have to be committed to them, and we prefer it if they're committed to us, but they don't have to be committed to the trade, especially not with Idoneus (more on that later—you're going to want to keep reading, especially if all this talk about commitment is making you feel nervous).

When you're worth many millions of dollars, you don't *have* to be committed to anything you don't want to be committed to. My job for more than two decades has been to *get* these clients committed; my job was to lead them to a place where they were committed, because if we didn't have two committed parties, we were very likely not going to make a successful trade. However, that was much more the case before the creation of

Idoneus. Before Idoneus, with the traditional asset trading model, you really were required to have two people committed at the same level at the same time, but today, because of newly available blockchain technology and our value exchange platform, this is not a requirement of value-for-value exchange. Today, if you are engaged and committed, you can now trade a million dollars in value or even hundreds of millions of dollars in value in days instead of decades. Let that sink in. A process that used to be like pulling teeth for so many is now easier, more secure, and more beneficial than you could ever imagine. But we will move on to Idoneus and the next era of value exchange soon. Just know that while two-party commitment was a requirement for asset exchange throughout history, thankfully, today the ability to move value nearly instantly in and out of any asset class is in your hands directly.

Historically, to make an asset exchange of any kind—whether it was the obsidian stone of our prehistoric ancestors or a decamillion-dollar hotel-resort in the 1980s, or any similar asset exchange attempt as late as 2017, you first had to have two highly committed parties with very reasonable states of mind and balanced value perceptions and expectations—hard to find. That has always been the greatest challenge with asset exchange: the need for two parties to agree on the value and specific asset terms at the same moment. Thankfully, we have been able to overcome this.

But again, I'm getting ahead of myself.

In Summary

Commitment is more than a promise. It's a principle the most effective business people live by, day in and day out, and a principle we take extremely seriously. My experience has taught me that when you are truly committed to your goal, whatever your goal might be, you can accomplish the impossible—not just because you want to, but because you have made yourself willing to move mountains in pursuit of your goals. There is nothing more powerful than commitment, and it lives in your fingertips.

Commitment is something rarer than ever in the business world, believe me, and this rarity creates great difficulty for many who are navigating challenging asset transactions through incredibly turbulent economic periods.

No matter how committed you are and appear to be to others, unfortunately, your *own* commitment only goes one way. How do you test others' commitment? How do you know if you can trust another person? When it comes to high-value transactions, how can you possibly determine if the elements of the deal are strong enough to get to the finish line? How can you be sure that your trade partner won't end up extracting value that is rightfully yours, souring the deal and ruining your confidence? How can you be sure your assets are secure and your value stays intact?

Trading high-value assets can be an intimidating thing. Going into your first asset trade can feel a bit like trying to get into the stock market for the first time but instead of starting with a modest amount, as was likely the case when you made your first market investment, an asset exchange is likely seven figures or more—which can be overwhelming, to say the least. There are a lot of people out there who are only in it for themselves, who want to squeeze every last drop out of you and that which you have of value, but it is possible to separate the wheat from the chaff.

Believe it or not, I have found reliable techniques my team and I now use daily to bypass the need to personally determine the trustworthiness of potential clients and exchange partners: specifically, Idoneus. But before the Idoneus platform was developed, I had to rely upon my personal ability and that of my team to determine the quality of potential clients and partners. These techniques I implemented worked consistently, and have saved me and my team countless amounts of time and money. I was like an early jeweler, testing the legitimacy of each fleck of "obsidian" that comes through my door—and I can teach you these tools of my trade. When conducting traditional asset trades, these tools can be the difference between success and expensive, or even dangerous, failure.

Allow me to show you.

Chapter Three

Fostering Integrity

*"If you have integrity, nothing else matters. If you don't
have integrity, nothing else matters."*
—*Alan K. Simpson*

Wouldn't it be great if we didn't have to make mistakes along the way? If everything always went smoothly, if we never met those kinds of people who were less than honest, who wasted our time and made us want to lose our minds?

Yes. That would be nice.

But then again, if that were true, we would never learn, would we? We would never grow. We would never look at where we are and see how we need to change, to improve—

not just personally, but in our businesses, our methods, our strategies.

Early on in my career, I was working with a client, a young entrepreneur who told me he was ready to complete the transaction. He had a nice property and some significant funds that he claimed he was "very" ready and able to trade for a yacht. Yacht trades are often some of my favorites to complete, so I was pretty excited about this transaction going through. The client was acting very nonchalant about the cash component, assuring us that we didn't have to worry. He had the cash, he insisted, and it wouldn't be a problem. He brought up bank accounts, lines of credit, this and that—he had a lot of bravado, a lot of ego. I noticed that ego right away, and obviously didn't like it, but I ignored it and continued with the transaction. I was still early on in my business, after all, and this kind of trade would have been a very nice addition to my track record.

Well, those of you who are seasoned in the world of business can probably see the end of this story coming from a mile away. After several weeks of work and having what I thought were both parties fully committed—the other party, the one that had the yacht, was definitely committed—we found out that, obviously, he did not actually have those lines of credit he claimed he did, or they were not usable for the pending transaction. Big surprise there. He didn't have the cash; he didn't have the resources. The trade was dead in the water, and the other client was certainly not happy—with the trade partner or with me.

From then on, the very first thing I do when I meet someone who is bragging about their ability is *verify* that ability. Typically, people who have great ability don't find a need to boast about it—in fact, they rarely even talk about it.

I didn't know that then, so I wasted valuable time setting up that "trade." I misjudged a client and wasted my own time; I wasted the other party's time—but thankfully, it has rarely happened again. It was a lesson well learned. Today, we validate and qualify every client from the beginning to make sure each potential transaction partner is in fact able to transact. At first, I was worried clients wouldn't like how we approached this— would they find us to be paranoid, untrusting, bureaucratic?— but as we implemented a very detailed KYC/AML application process, we found that clients loved that we were doing our due diligence, not only on them but on every party we facilitate a trade with. It has served me well. As a result, not only do I not have to deal with those kinds of braggadocious clients, but we also have far fewer mistakes and far fewer misjudgments.

When I started the company that would grow into the foundation of our global asset trading firm, I had to learn, very quickly and effectively, how to read people and determine their character. I had to learn how to determine whether the person I was talking to shared my values or if they were just out to cause problems or waste my valuable time—or, worst of the worst, scam us and our client(s) out of hard-earned money and assets.

But how do you know what people value? How do you know if they share your values? How do you know if they will keep their word, or if they'll leave you high and dry? How do you know if they'll be fair, or try to take advantage of you?

The answer: you do your due diligence. Every time. Without exception.

Best Practices

Work in this field is not just about researching the best island for windsurfing—it requires researching the clients themselves. We can't take on everyone who walks through our door, which is something you can probably relate to, if you are the kind of high-value individual who would be interested in this book. I often turn away from potential clients or transactions that don't suit my code of ethics, or just feel wrong for one reason or another.

I've been telling a lot of stories from early in my career, but this is something that still holds true today. Even now, with Idoneus, we often come across very substantial estates—castles, private islands, etc. We come across them, we acquire them, we own them, we trade them, we manage them, and we get offered many different ways to drive revenue with those properties in the meantime. One of the times I was offered to do so was with a 16-bedroom estate. The idea that was presented to us was to fill this gorgeous estate with—shall we say, "very attractive attendees," if you follow me there. For hundreds of thousands of dollars a month, this person wanted to cycle in "models" from around the world, starting with that estate and then growing to 10 or 12 estates. Let's just say this wasn't for a fashion show, okay? I know, it's not pretty, but this is a real thing that happened, and it's the kind of thing you can see a lot in the high-dollar, high-value space. It's probably something you've heard about happening, if you're in these spheres—and if you're the kind of client we'd want to work with, this is something you equally didn't want to get involved in. Sometimes people—people who don't have much—think that the more money you have, the fewer morals you need. I don't believe that's true at all. In fact, it is quite the opposite in reality.

When people come to me offering ideas like this that could perhaps generate a lot of profit but don't fit my personal code of ethics, I simply decline and move on. I don't want to get involved in that which is even questionable, much less illegal. I don't want to get involved in anything that is technically legal but is still not of integrity or not in line with my personal values. Even with that example above—while I wouldn't have been "in" that business, I would have been providing the asset to people who are in that business, and that's not an involvement I would be proud of. My personal policy is that I never want to be in a business that—God forbid, if I were to pass away and my daughter had to become involved in my affairs—my daughter would be disappointed by. I don't want to get mixed up in anything even slightly questionable. I never want to be in a situation where I'm not above reproach.

That's just how I approach business. Sometimes, determining whether or not to do something or get involved in something, determining whether or not it's a good idea—it's just an instinct. Early on in my asset trading career, I worked with a client who I felt right away wasn't trustworthy. His first red flag was that he didn't treat the women in our company with the same respect with which he treated the men, and anyone who isn't fair to all humans equally, I have found, is less likely to be fair to *you* in business as well. Looking back, there were several red flags. Regardless, I decided—perhaps against my better judgment—to move forward on a transaction with him anyway. Well, I learned my lesson. He was one of only a few people in the company's history to go behind our backs to try to hurt us.

I met him at one of his very large estates in Europe one night while in the process of negotiating our trade, and that night, I actually had to intervene between him and his son. He was intoxicated and chasing his son around the house—his son was about eight or nine years old and scared to death of his father at that moment. I was able to separate them and get his son away from the situation. I actually put his son—who I just met that day—to bed. Then I had to go calm down the client, a man worth hundreds of millions of dollars, who was drunk beyond belief. A truly disappointing evening.

We had already shown him an asset that was potentially a fit. It was a 30-million-dollar trade on each side. A 60-million-dollar asset trade would have been very big for us, for anyone at that time. The introduction was made before I knew any of this about him, about his character, about his behavior around women and even around his own child. It wasn't until after the trade was beginning to be set into motion when I was invited to his home and saw how he acted in private, with his family.

At that moment, if this happened today, I would have walked away and said, "I don't do business with people who behave in this manner. Our interests are not aligned. Thank you. Have a nice night." But at that time, earlier in my career, I just kind of set it aside and moved forward. As you probably know, someone who treats women and children poorly, well, it's only a matter of time before they treat *you* just as poorly. We had already worked out an initial agreement between two parties, initiated several transatlantic trips, introduced the assets and signed a formal MOU—we were well on our way to completing a massive trade of two iconic properties. I just wanted to get this trade done and over with, and it seemed like we were close to doing so.

In the end, he pulled the rug out from under us. He decided he was going to try to go *direct* with the other client, to "cut out the middleman" (us) and try to avoid our multimillion-dollar fee—a fee that we had earned, since *we* had done all the hard work! Now we weren't going to be paid a penny for all that work, but there was nothing we could do. Well, he went off and tried to do the trade on his own, but these two parties were very, very different kinds of people. They had different values, different communication styles, and did not go well together—

which was why our role as the go-between *existed*, but I digress. He blew the deal up, losing value for himself, losing value for the other client, and of course, losing value for us. So now, when we see that kind of behavior in a client, we don't ignore it. We don't say it's "not our business," and go ahead with the business anyway, because before long, something that is "not our business" often affects our business. Now, we take it deeply into consideration and typically choose not to work with any clients that go so deeply against our own values.

Long story short, I don't make that mistake anymore. When people tell you who they are, believe them. When you have a strong feeling about someone, don't ignore it, no matter what. You don't have to act on it right away, by any means, but you shouldn't throw caution to the wind—especially when it concerns your assets and your hard-earned value.

Hopefully, you are reading this and nodding your head in total agreement—but if you're sweating under the collar, wondering how you're going to hide this or that less-than-honorable aspect of yourself or your business when you give us a call . . . you probably shouldn't call us.

I've grown to find that integrity is fostered within, and respect is earned. You can gain respect by having integrity and by treating others with respect. I have used this to my advantage, as I have shown, but this is a two-way street. Especially as I have gained a reputation and become established in my field, I stopped taking every client who shook my hand just for the paycheck—and when I get a good client, I don't take the first deal that walks through the door, even if they're anxiously pressing for a trade. Today, I am very selective. I don't just have to earn their respect; they have to earn mine. This has, though it may seem counterintuitive, made our organization a much more sought-after company. No, I don't take everyone, and no, I'm not a doormat, but I am fair, and people respect that. I have values, and people respect that. I have boundaries, and when people respect my boundaries, I respect them in return, and we're both happy. If a client does not respect me, my time, or my team, I no longer feel the need to bend over backward for them. This has been a much healthier practice for both myself and our companies.

Whenever possible, I try to meet people in person before doing significant business with them. It is important to me to be able to watch someone's body language, to hear how they speak, and to connect with them in person. There is a deep, inherent connection that can only happen when two humans are present in the same room, at the same table. I just can't get the full story when we're both sitting in our comfortable at-home offices on the telephone or in an online meeting—I need to see if their hands are fidgeting, if they have trouble making eye contact, if they give a firm or hesitant handshake. I need to see how they handle social pressure, and I need to know for certain that they are cutting me off out of rudeness, not solely because of Zoom's bad connection. This has become more difficult in the recent pandemic years, when many of us were trapped in one place, but regardless, meeting people in person is always preferable to meeting people online or over the phone—even in today's high-tech world. I like to speak with them, to see how they interact with me, with my team— even with the waitstaff at the restaurant we might meet at.

How someone treats those they see as "lesser" than them can speak volumes about their integrity—and how they'll treat you in turn, as your client or as your trade partner. Do they tip well? Personally, I would find it *very* telling if they leave zero gratuity to an excellent server while discussing a multimillion-dollar deal, or if they yelled at him/her for getting something wrong due to a purely innocent mistake. Do they treat the server kindly, or are they making inappropriate jokes or advances? Do they make small talk, or do they pretend they don't even hear them? All these things can tell you more about a person before you even begin to talk business.

Another telling tactic is to ask about their families. Are they invested in their children, or do they struggle to remember what grade they're in? Do they respect and support their spouse, or do they degrade them, or even resent them, and let you know about it the first time you meet them? If you are operating in the high-value sector, you will want to work with people who are respectful and honest. I have found that the more connected they are with their own family and/or close sphere, the more likely it is that they will be connected and fair when working with you and with their trade partner.

One potential client, as I mentioned, treated some of the women on our staff less than respectfully, and I regret ever even considering doing business with him. He went into our business dealings expecting the world—the best deal, the highest value—and he went into it expecting to be able to treat me and my team like the ground he walked on. That doesn't work for us—and it doesn't work for my valued connections, either. Even if I did take on a client like that, I probably couldn't close a trade, since no one else would want to work with them! On top of that, future clients might not want to work with me, since I saw all those red flags and marched right onward anyway.

This world of value is about so much more than dollar signs and glittering gold. It's about character. It's about *integrity, the core ingredient of our personal value.*

Let me encourage you to pay close attention to the people you are working with, because your future clients and associates are paying attention, too. You do not want to be known as "the person who worked with so-and-so," when so-and-so takes a very poor action which becomes public or stirs up a controversial media scandal over a less-than-desirable subject matter. You want to vet the people you work with, the people you trade with, and the people you befriend, especially in today's media-crazed, constantly online society. This is also why, by the way, I am so protective of my own online presence. What makes it online will be discoverable there forever, so I am always working to be diligent to make sure myself and my business are presented and viewed in as clear and professional a manner as my valued clientele. Fortunately, if we do ever work together, our team will manage this trade partner qualifying process for you, so you can rely on us to make sure your trade business only goes to someone you (and we) can trust.

Considerate and Thorough

We take a customized approach to value, since not everyone values the same things. Instead, we ask questions—or better yet, like with the windsurfer, we do our research ahead of time and come prepared before they can even lift a finger in doubt. While we endeavor to treat everyone with an equal amount of respect and kindness, we don't treat everyone as if they are the same.

Of course, when we receive a lead on a potential client, we research everything we can about what they are looking for, the asset or other form of value they are offering to trade to get it, and who they are as a person. It would be a pretty bad experience if I went into a trade with, say, Cristiano Ronaldo and didn't know he was one of the world's greatest football players. When going into any transaction, I also always try to determine, if I can, whether I share values with this person *before* I start going into business discussions with them. I do my research, which is part of what has made me stand out in this field. In today's short-attention-span society, it is more impressive than ever when one remembers the details they learned about another person. Remembering someone's children's names can be the difference between us and another potential company earning the client's business. We understand the value of knowing our customer and knowing what they value above all else.

Bite the Gold Medal

I'm sure you've watched the Olympics before. It's amazing to watch these talented people take home those medals, isn't it? Have you ever noticed how, when the winner gets the gold medal, they often bite it?

Have you ever wondered why?

Turns out, it's an age-old method of testing the quality of gold to make sure it is real. Gold is soft, but not too soft. If you bite it, it will not break, but you will leave teeth marks indented into it. (Don't try this at home. I'm not responsible for any dented—or, worse, *undented*—jewelry!)

This method has been around long before complex tools were developed for testing gold, but it still works today on solid gold, and it is an easy way to help determine the true worth of this metal—or those medals.

While I wouldn't suggest biting your trading partner—or the wing of their multimillion-dollar aircraft—I do a similar "bite test" when determining someone's quality as a person and as a businessperson.

When meeting with them, I ask myself questions like these:

- Do they seem to put compensation above value?
- Do they seem more wishy-washy and hesitant than committed?

- Do they insist on an NDA right out of the gate?
- Are they nickel and diming?
- Do they seem suspicious of our true motives, even paranoid?
- Do they treat me poorly?
- Do they treat people on my team who they view as lower than me in the hierarchy poorly?
- Do they treat people in public—waitstaff, the receptionist, people on the street—poorly?
- Do they expect me to pick up the check without discussion?
- Do they disrespect my time—showing up late, leaving early, not coming at all?
- Do they reschedule over and over again, especially for reasons like, "I forgot I had _____ today"?
- Do they seem disconnected to me and to the moment?
- Do they keep checking their watch—or worse, their phone?
- When I ask about their family, do they seem uninvested or even uninterested in them?
- Do they keep interrupting me or changing the subject?
- Do they forget basic personal details about me, maybe even my name?

If I find myself checking off a lot of those boxes, they've probably failed the bite test. High-value people with significant assets don't need to take advantage of you—in my experience, it's typically the lower value people who will. It's often the classic old-money-versus-new-money trope happening here, but that isn't always the case, either. Everyone is different, and the only way you can determine the value of a connection is by actually connecting with them.

You may be surprised to learn, in the list above, that I generally dislike NDAs. Nondisclosure agreements are, to me, a sign that people don't trust. Untrustworthy people are more likely to distrust other people—it's classic projection. If someone hands me an NDA, they are saying that they automatically see me as a potential enemy, and expect me to do something to hurt them if this deal goes poorly. Well, if that's what they're projecting, that is likely exactly what they would do to me. I now try to steer clear of the paranoid. There are exceptions to this rule, but they are few and far between.

Of course, I can also "bite test" the asset they want to trade, as well. Depending on the asset at hand, there are a few secret and not-so-secret ways to determine its true value.

Here are some tests of quality and marketability that I often employ when initially determining asset quality/value.

1. Traditional Market Value Method: a good starting point but really is more opinion than anything else and must be supported by other indicators of marketability and value.

2. Cost of Creation Method: not to be overlooked or underestimated. Can it be created again? If so, how easily, how quickly, and for how much? Or is it one of a kind? This is a seemingly simple point that often is overlooked and many times is one of the most impactful factors to determine marketability.

3. Average Time of Sale: knowing this single factor of value will save you from making potential seriously painful acquisition errors. Many parties speak about the value of assets but not the time frame that will be required to achieve that value in the open market. This is a primary focus for me when evaluating any asset and should be for you as well!

In Summary

Many things have value, but even some things that look identical to the naked eye can have vastly different true values. Look at a master painting next to a forgery—one is worthless, the other worth millions, but they are seemingly identical to the untrained eye. Or a million-dollar natural diamond next to a lab-created diamond, moissanite, or cubic zirconia. It can take the trained eye of a master to determine true value. While you can do various "bite tests" and try to determine the value of your trading partners and their assets on your own, it's easier— and safer—to engage a professional to walk you through this most difficult part of the process. Delegate, as you do in your core business, and let highly skilled professionals do the hard work for you.

By the time I founded my first asset trading firm, I had built a successful model that, in and of itself, had tremendous value. I, like you and many of my clients, was now in possession of something very unique and valuable if managed properly, and I was now focused on development and diversification. How was this value going to evolve in the future? Going to change? Going to improve?

The answer: in ways beyond my imagination.

PART TWO

EXCHANGING VALUE

Chapter Four

What is Value?

"How you define and pursue value will determine more about your success or failure than any other factor in your life."
—Jarrett Preston

I probably don't have to tell you that "value" is not synonymous with "price" and it's not synonymous with "money," but what might surprise you to hear is that value is *also* not always synonymous with "assets." Many things, beyond those that have a price tag attached to them, have tremendous value. It's all a matter of perspective.

Value, in other words, is in the eye of the beholder.

Money

When we are first taught about value—I am referring to when we are just children—we are taught about money. Cash. Dollar bills, Euros, Pound Sterling, etc. So, it is natural that as we get older, the idea of cash is seductive. Do you remember your first paycheck? Or the first time the nice neighbors gave you a 10-dollar bill for shoveling the snow in the driveway? Personally, I certainly do. I don't know about you, but for me, it felt amazing to have some dollars in my pocket that were all mine to spend as I saw fit.

However, cash isn't what it used to be—and I mean that on both a micro scale and on a macro scale.

Remember earlier, when I discussed how trade began many thousands of years ago, and how we have proved the existence of extensive trade networks via the tracking of obsidian? It was actually these massive trade networks that made money a necessary invention. Indeed, this is why the definition of money is that it is a *medium of trade*—it is a method through which trade can occur smoothly and effectively. Money is a medium of trade the way oil paints are a medium of art. We'll come back to this.

Early money was not made of paper like it is today. In fact, the earliest "coins" were cowrie shells, salt, livestock, grain, and beads. Indeed, in some parts of South Sudan, livestock are still used as a method of currency today. Money actually is older than written language—we have evidence of tally-marked sticks being used as an accounting tool; in effect, as money—as far back as 30,000 years ago. In Egypt, there are ancient storehouses of clay tablets, each thousands of years old—worthless, unless they were some sort of money. And the good old metal coin has been found across the globe in several ancient cultures as well, from Chinese coins with holes in the center for easy stringing to Roman coins, which had the stamped head of state on the currency, a practice many countries still take part in today.

The main benefit of money is that the parties using it don't have to have a direct trade of tangible value between them. If you have grain to trade with for an obsidian blade, but the merchant says you don't have enough, you can make up the difference with coins. If you don't want an obsidian blade, but do want to sell your grain, you can trade with the obsidian merchant for their coins, which you can then use to trade with someone else to get something you do actually want. It's a simple and elegant solution, which is probably why it has cropped up in one form or another in nearly every civilization, going back through recorded history. So long as you can get everyone to agree that a piece of metal, or some paper, or a pretty seashell is worth something, you've established an economy.

Money is so old and so consistent across cultures, you may question how quickly and easily I shrug it off as not important. Of course, money is not *un*important; it is still necessary to live. Your electric bill can't be paid with jewels and yachts or grains of rice, after all. But, it is my advice and the advice of many of the world's foremost experts to only keep as much cash as you need to operate, and not a penny more.

Go back further, before money, and you will see the truth of the matter: money does not actually make trade easier. It might seem like money solves the issue of questioning how much *grain* an obsidian blade is worth, but all it does is bring up the question of how much *money* an obsidian blade is worth. Note the very important difference. The obsidian merchant can take advantage of you, whether you're trading grain or coin.

Remember, money is a *medium of trade.* It is worthless, besides—as worthless as those Egyptian clay tablets would be to us today. What's worth more: oil paints, or a masterpiece created from those paints? Exactly.

And to be frank, using money today as a medium of trade is like using honey as a medium of swimming. Slow, and terribly inefficient.

Money, above all else, is inconsistent. Its value is reliant on politics and inflation, and both of those are out of control (and spiraling even more out of control as we speak). Money is trash. Look at it—really look at it closely. All money really is, is colored paper! Those Egyptian hunks of clay are worthless today—but their golden artifacts aren't! Money has no inherent value, the way a solid asset does. An asset retains value over the years—in some cases, over the centuries. What is the lesson here? When it is required, you need to move in and out of money as quickly as possible, or you will end up watching it all crumble to dust.

So, if money has no value, what *does* have value? Let's take a look at something that has, perhaps, the most value of all.

Time

Time is a uniquely valuable asset. In fact, it's arguably the *most* valuable asset, and just like physical assets, time is something we can trade and invest. Most of the population trade their time for an hourly wage or annual salaries paid in money. When a new lawyer, real estate professional, or doctor is starting out in their career, they typically do not value their personal time nearly as much as they value their work (and the income and prestige that comes with it), so they often devote all the time they have to their profession. As they get older, their priorities tend to shift. Perhaps now they want to focus on their health, or—as is extremely common—on their families. They often work less in later years of their career, since personal time is now of premium value to them over income or career achievements. Spending more time doing what they love becomes more important to them than earning more income or gaining more career achievements.

What stage of life are you in? Is this sounding more and more familiar, as you get older, as you advance in your career and your success?

Many people, after the first or second stage of their careers, reach a point where their time is indeed more valuable than money. While at first they would work overtime, constantly, for a few extra dollars, or learn how to repair their vehicle or other such items to avoid purchasing new items or services, they've now reached the point where paying someone else to do these tasks for them is a better, smarter decision. This is why the wealthy sometimes have multiple housekeepers or other personal staff, right? It's not that they are too good to vacuum the rugs—it's that they have less time than they do money, and vacuuming, dusting, or taking care of their 12-bedroom mansion all take time. They are not lazy, not in the slightest. They just realize they can use that very valuable time to do something they have deemed as more worthy of their time, more important for either themselves personally or their business. The cost of a housekeeper is less than the cost of losing those hours to pushing a vacuum around, so while it may seem a superfluous waste of value to those who cannot afford a housekeeper or opt not to hire them, it is actually anything but.

Valuing time is a sign of maturity and security.

Relationships

On the subject of maturity, it's important to note that relationships themselves are immensely valuable—especially relationships that are nurtured and allowed to blossom into maturity. Obviously, people value their relationships with their families, spouses, and loved ones, but these aren't the only relationships that hold significant and real value—and they are certainly not the only relationships that you will want to nurture.

There is a client I have who, to date, after years of effort, still owns an asset I have not been able to complete a transaction for—admittedly, not for lack of trying. I've been "on the terrace," as we say, with this person, and we've come very close to trading his 40-million-dollar asset on multiple occasions, but for one reason or another, we have not yet made it to a closing. I have met with him in multiple countries to discuss the subject and present offers, two, three times, even a fourth time, expending substantial resources to do so, and still have not ended up closing a deal with him. Some people might get frustrated by this point—just writing the whole thing off as a failure and giving up. They might stop calling, stop visiting, stop being so polite or engaged at functions and fundraisers when we come across each other. They might decide that this person is "too flaky" or noncommittal and/or "not worth their time."

That may be the case for them. But it is not the case for me. I don't only value relationships that expand my wallet, because I know sometimes the *relationship* is the actual value I am receiving. While it's true, I might be able to close more business or possibly generate quicker returns if I refocus my energy away from this person and work with a more willing-to-sell client in the hours I spend with him, but I have realized long ago that relationships can be worth far more than a few extra depreciating dollars in the bank.

This relationship in particular has proven that fact to me more than any other business relationship I've ever had. Yes, I've been working on and off for years without closing this specific transaction for this person, but we have closed other business and in the process have become very close friends. In fact, we are truly great friends—he has even taken on something of a "father figure" and advisor role in my life, at times giving me the kind of priceless wisdom and strong mentorship I missed out on during several years of my youth when my own father was not present. His wisdom has been more valuable to me than any payday, especially for someone like me who has had to forge his own path in the business world from the beginning. I can call this person—who built his very successful empire from nothing—at any time to seek his advice on important decisions in my life or business. Seriously—back when speed dial was common, he was on my speed dial, and nearly first on my list of valuable advisors to call! That's something I never would have gained had I given up after failing to close on the initial asset exchange we started on. In fact, this person spent many hours advising me when I was first working to plan and create our current venture (Idoneus). His guidance has been invaluable to me personally and to every person we work with. I can't thank him enough.

He's not the only one, either. My phone is full of contacts of extraordinary people, who I can call upon for business or personal advice at any time. If I have questions about the economy, market conditions, peculiar market forces, or any other economic or business question, I have open access to some of the brightest minds on Earth. I can't express how helpful this has been, during countless moments of my business career and personal life. They'll pick up the phone if they see it's me calling—and if they can't speak at that exact moment, they'll call me back. Guaranteed. They're not just "clients" who might answer my questions for a discount on future services—they're loyal friends, and they're the kind of friends who will *want* to help me, not for something in return, but because they value my friendship and want to see me succeed, just like any other friend would do. Some of them I've closed business with, but many of them I haven't. We've talked about potential trades, or we've met up and chatted over dinner and sometimes ended up avoiding business talk altogether. Their friendship, wisdom, and relationship with me is more valuable than anything else.

Of course, I'd be misleading you if I said their wisdom and company were the only benefits from our continued friendship. If they ever do decide to sell or trade their assets and need a capable professional, I have no doubt that I'll be the first person they call. And if their friends or associates ever need someone in my arena, I know they'll recommend them to me as they often have. If you're in a high-stakes business like me, you know how vital word of mouth is, and thanks to them, I have gained access to one of the world's most exclusive and high-value networks ever made. Not only am I their friend, but they've seen me in action, by this point, many times. They've been a part of countless stories of success, and many have even advised on strategies to help me succeed for others, and they know my successes firsthand. Building this type of network is the backbone of business, and it's important to keep that backbone strong and healthy.

Information

Relationships are valuable, and information, wisdom, and advice from mentors are all valuable, as we've discussed, but so are other types of information—such as scientific discoveries. On a personal basis, I once was working with a scientist as a business advisor. He was working on a significant medical science development that could help millions of people fighting a deadly illness—a highly valuable asset indeed. He offered to pay for our advisory services up front out of capital raised, but instead I suggested that he hold the funds. Save the money, continue to invest it in his research, and we would find value later. Why? The information this person had to share with the world was far more important than any fee we might be paid on the front end. We made an agreement where, instead of upfront payment, we would be compensated once the invention was on the market serving society. The information was far too valuable to risk delaying product development by deploying critical capital to early-stage compensation. I knew in this scenario that patience would return the most value for all parties. This is often the case but difficult to realize in the moment, unless you have the experience to draw upon.

For a more common example, look at formal schooling. Colleges and universities are often framed as "investments," with the conceit of those institutions being that going to them will result in a higher paying job further down the line. While it is true that many people leave with a degree that, while expensive, has given them a treasure trove of information and propels them into a career that easily pays them back for their trouble. Of course, this is not always the case—there are countless stories of people who never use their college degree, or who have trouble paying back their loans when the paycheck they expected as starry-eyed freshmen isn't the paycheck they get as entry-level graduates. As always, every investment must be weighed against risk and potential future returns. I'm not the kind of person who would advise to drop half a million dollars on a degree in musical theater that isn't likely to get me a stable stream of income—let's put it that way.

Smaller investments into information can be in the form of courses or even books like the one you are reading right now. You didn't buy this book so you could own a couple hundred pieces of paper; no doubt you bought this book for the information within it because you believed it might help you in the long run. Keep that in mind when you begin thinking outside the box about what truly counts as real "assets," and real value because they are often different than you might expect. Understanding and having the ability to calculate value in its raw form is something that we benefit from in every aspect of life.

I am the Value

However important it is to form relationships because of their inherent value to you, you must keep in mind that value cannot be a one-way street. Anyone with a successful marriage can attest to this statement: good relationships are built on give and take, and that's true in business, too. You have to provide as much value to them as your counterparty provides to you. This value may not be in the same form, but it must be comparably equal nonetheless. That level of equivalent exchange is the best way to increase your success rate—in any relationship, business or personal.

My clients know, because I have proven over the years, that I am reliable. I get them the results they want where others have failed. It may take time, negotiation, and creativity, but I always deliver—and I always get the value I ask for in return, because they know I am worth what I ask for. I have inherent value. This position I enjoy today is due to what we've gone over already—the building blocks of integrity and commitment, combined with a healthy dose of deep networking and relationship building that many others ignore.

When someone engages my services, they may be in a good place and simply want to trade one asset for another that is a better fit. However, they may instead be in a more precarious situation—or, as is more and more often the case in today's economy, they may be *in danger of falling into* a very precarious situation. Remember the client of mine we discussed in the introduction who had to be airlifted by helicopter from the roof of his mansion due to unexpected destabilization of the country resulting in dangerous riots and attacks on the local wealthy population? Or the family who had to move their family and their assets from their war-torn home country in a matter of days due to a true life-or-death situation? They each had to start over with practically nothing, despite their prior fortune built over a 25- to 30-year period. They were intelligent people. They were successful. They thought they were safe, they thought it could never happen to them. They were wrong. It did happen to them, and it could happen to any of us, even you.

Being worried about this sort of thing isn't paranoia; it's just being realistic and honest about what is happening in the world we are living in. We are in uncharted territory in many ways, fiscally, socially, politically, and economically.

Those who have been paying attention to the hectic landscape of today know the importance of having someone they can trust when it comes to securing their assets and protecting their future. I've certainly been paying attention over these past two-plus decades—and I've seen many suffer the consequences when they assumed they were safe and in the clear, managing their assets in the same traditional manner as previous generations. The world has changed in major ways recently, as I'm sure you're aware, and I've been keeping my finger on the pulse of these changes, watching them closely, and adjusting my practices accordingly. I've become that trustworthy person who can offer the kind of solutions you hope you will never need. You can be certain that when the news starts getting sour, a large percentage of the world's most successful people out there will be memorizing our web address, and I and my team will be ready. We've seen it when businesses began failing in 2008, we saw it again during the pandemic, and when war hit Ukraine, and we'll see it again when the next tragedy begins to unfold, wherever it may be.

I know very well that the value of the services my team and I deliver can at times be the difference of life or death. It can be the difference between a family continuing to live a life of secure luxury or enduring a highly impactful financial loss that can make it difficult to make ends meet—yes, even for those who today are multimillionaires and beyond. If you're still rolling your eyes in assumption that this could never happen to you, or because you think even if it did, it would never be as bad as I'm making it out to be, you need a reality check, my dear friend. It can happen, and if the stars align, it *will* happen. I have had a client worth $100 million pick me up in their private jet for our first business trip together and 24 months later have had that same client ask me if I could cover his rental car costs after landing from a commercial flight because he had nothing left and was in the fight of his life to recover.

I am also aware that because of the anxiety that such situations create and the magnitude of these decisions, many potential clients may hesitate to create a strategy at all for divesting of unneeded or unwanted assets, or may choose to follow the direction of traditional advisors who are not aware of the value preservation methods our team has refined at

Idoneus. One must have a thick skin in a business like this, so we don't get angry or upset when a client chooses not to work with us, changes their mind, or goes a completely different direction. We take rejection in stride and still send holiday cards because we know that this relationship can be extremely valuable to both parties in the future. And when those clients return to us, as they often do, we simply smile and get to work, picking up right where we left off to create and implement a strategy to successfully move them out of one form of value into another that meets their needs for the future.

Key Takeaways

Value is more than assets and cash. Yes, a handful of zeros in the bank account is wonderful, but one solid ally in this business or a few weeks of quality time with your family can be worth far more. In particular, high-quality relationships, information, and time can be worth more than even the purest gold. When you think of the word "value," think outside the box.

I have learned over my years in business that if I can show people that I see value in their relationship with me, they will respect me for it and will often provide value in return. However, I also learned that I have to prove my worth. You can not preach "dignity" and "respect," then get emotional and refuse to be kind or responsive when someone decides not to work with you. Some of my most valued relationships are with people who declined my services on multiple occasions—

people I've, on paper, never made a cent with. However, their advice and wisdom has multiplied my business and quality of life in ways that are incalculable. Sometimes you won't get a paycheck, but you will still get paid in dividends. Value is built on the foundation of relationships (as is life), so make sure your relationships are genuine and healthily beneficial to both or all sides. Equivalent exchange is a major tenet of value-for-value exchange, and it starts at the relationship level.

Something doesn't have to be identical or in the same form to hold comparable value. In fact, you are never going to be able to exchange something with an exact copy—otherwise, the trade would be pointless. Capitalism is based on the idea of trading money for goods and services, after all—if we were just trading money for money, it wouldn't make any sense, right? This is also why I am personally not a fan of the speculative cryptocurrency trading we have seen so much of in recent years. Remember, *the value is in between*. Think of the parent who takes a pay cut or works fewer hours to spend more time with their children. Sure, they have less money, but they have more of what they value most: time with their children and family.

The smartest among us may be wealthy, but they don't get swept up into the world of money. They don't let greed sneak in, and they don't become blinded by the allure of cash. I know, believe me, it feels great to see high numbers in the bank account, but cash, very candidly, is one of the worst asset classes available to us today. If you're reading this book and in the world of assets or value trading at all, you know that already, but it can still hypnotize the best of us at times. Consider this your warning bell to break free of dependence on cash. Those who do this earliest will achieve the greatest gains as the modern financial economy continues to take shape.

You've heard me say before that cash may be king, but even the strongest and healthiest kings can be put into checkmate. If most of your wealth is held in the bank or stock markets, well, be reminded of what happened to the entire country of Greece between 2008 and 2010, or to those heavily invested with Lehman Brothers in 2008, or to the Russians in early 2022—or, for that matter, the whole world during the Great Depression. Banks can close, the stock market can crash, inflation can blow up like a balloon, and there goes the life savings. However, real estate is real estate, gold is gold, and diamonds are diamonds. The market can fluctuate, but these things will hold substantial value over time, no matter what inflation or the banks do to the U.S. dollar or other popular fiat currencies. *Assets* are really in charge, so if you're still relying heavily on dollar bills or other fiat currency, seriously consider breaking this habit and turn toward a focus on asset classes that truly serve you.

If that scares you, we can help you. You'll be glad we did.

To be very candid, I don't see cash as "valuable" at all beyond amounts required for basic needs/function. I may have early in my career, but this lesson is one I learned very quickly in this business. When it comes down to it, cash has far too many downsides, too many risks. Rather, I see cash as solely one (not the only) path to the real valuable commodity: assets. I highly suggest you try to view it in the same way, at least while we take this journey of value together.

And remember: "assets" are not only things like property, diamonds, art and gold, but also time, information, and relationships. Sure, you could spend many hours or even months—however long it would take—to learn how to repair the transmission in your Ferrari 812 Superfast, and you could get it done for "just the cost of parts." *Alternatively*, you could spend a little money to have an expert do it. Yes, you lose some money, but you gain time and a perfectly repaired Ferrari *and* the peace of mind that it was done correctly.

Information, in the form of wisdom, can be more valuable than anything on the planet. That scientist's information was worth more than our advance payment, which is why we approached that project in the way we did. The Ferrari repairman in the example above has the information you need, and that information has value.

Truly ask yourself, "What do I value?" Try to detach your answer from the answer your family, friends, and culture expect you to say, and get down to the honest answer. If you're spending significant amounts of time doing things you don't want to do just to save money, you might need to change your approach. If what you value is not where you are directing the majority of your time, assets, and capital, consider a re-evaluation. Consider calling me. The certified Ferrari mechanic can do a realignment on your car, and we can do a realignment and reallocation of the things you truly value. This is especially important when determining how to manage a lifetime of assets collected that now may not fit your current or future values and goals.

How long has it been since you had a check-in on your values? I invite you to take a few minutes to consider where you place the greatest value in your life and how your value is currently diversified. Ask yourself the following questions, and sincerely contemplate the honest answers for each of them:

- Where do you invest the greatest amount of time and energy currently?
- Where would you *prefer* to invest the greatest amount of time and energy, if you do not do so already?
- Where are you investing capital and financial resources that you would benefit from redirecting elsewhere?
- What assets do you currently own that no longer meet your needs and goals?
- What strategies might you consider implementing to divest in a beneficial manner and re-distribute your holdings to assets that better suit you?

In Summary

I know what you're thinking, and no—I am not in the business of convincing someone to trade their multimillion-dollar estates for "time" and "relationships" alone. That would have me out of this business pretty quickly! At the end of the day, any asset trade needs to be a win-win situation for everyone involved.

Value comes in many forms, which can be intimidating and difficult to parse for someone who isn't in the business of doing so. If you're reading this from the aft deck of your second superyacht and you just can't seem to sell your first one, you already know that. It can be hard, taxing, and draining to try to trade assets in a way that *doesn't* result in a huge headache or many times a huge loss for one party or the other. It's hard to agree on the value of something, and harder still to get that value in exchange for it. It's difficult to work up the energy to barter with people who seem untrustworthy, and it's even more difficult to find people willing to barter at all. Finding buyers is hard, getting them to close is harder, and even then, if you succeed in setting up a trade, there's often miles of red tape and confusion to wade through (depending on one's asset and the legal jurisdiction and depending on the countries of origin of both trade partners). In these scenarios, often one side settles and gets less than what they deserve, just so the whole ordeal can be over and done with.

However, my experience has taught me that valuable assets *can* be exchanged in a win-win scenario, without having to go through the red-tape middleman of cash. I don't want you to settle, and I want you to avoid all the headaches and financial pressures this process can bring. I can do this for you. This is my specialty.

Have I caught your attention? Good.

Let's move on to my favorite part and discuss the all-important methods of exchanging one valuable asset for another.

Chapter Five

Trading Value

"Inaccessible value is of no value at all."
—*Jarrett Preston*

Remember the story of the family in the introduction? The family that had it all, but then lost it when they had to leave their home quickly in a time of dangerous revolt against the wealthy in the region? Well, believe it or not, they're a real family, a family I worked with. And yes, this really happened to them. They were going to sell, but couldn't find a buyer, so they were stuck, trying to enjoy their expensive assets but not really loving what they had. They sat on that property for years, waiting for a miracle buyer, ignoring the dangerous stories in the news, figuring it would never happen to them.

Then, the violence *did* reach their property lines and they were suddenly forced to evacuate, leaving all their precious assets behind. Their net worth plummeted in the span of 15 minutes. They possessed a lot of value, like you may, but much of it was "trapped" in their assets, seemingly without an easy path out. Once they had to evacuate their mansion, leaving it—and all those valuables—behind, it was all gone. Stolen, sold off, burned. They had to start virtually all over—no more long summer vacations or weekends on the yacht with their children for a long while.

If you've built yourself up from the bottom, you know how hard this is. This family had already done it once, reaching what is for many seemingly unreachable heights in wealth and prosperity. The idea of doing it all a second time seemed even more impossible than doing it the first time.

The family had tried to sell multiple assets before disaster struck, including the mansion, but were simply not able to. Many want to live in a castle, after all, but nobody wants to pay for it— and the carry costs are unbelievable. So, let's back away from the worst-case scenario, for a moment. Even if the dangerous revolt hadn't happened, they would have very likely been stuck with that property for years, trying to sell it, being forced to renovate it and pay the expensive carry costs on it, fruitlessly waiting for someone to give them approximately what they paid for it. And now it needs a new kitchen, and maybe another bathroom will make it more appealing, and it's time to pay someone to open up the pool again—even if you don't want to swim in it, it looks good for buyers, so you have to do it. And the management fees and the taxes are rising, and after several seasons, you need all new soft goods, draperies, etc., and on and on it goes.

Well, they never found a buyer, so on top of all those upkeep and renovation costs, they paid the ultimate price on that one: losing it all, and getting nothing in return but a truckload of trauma.

The family from the introduction had some cash, which many people call "liquid assets." Yes, that was helpful, as they were able to survive in the time to come, but as we'll discuss soon, cash holdings as the backup plan isn't ideal, either. Banks can close, economies can tank, and even something seemingly solid—like the U.S. dollar—can become nearly worthless before you can say "bankrupt." You are probably familiar with stories of German families papering their walls with German currency after it became nearly worthless after the first World War, or the insane inflation in countries like Venezuela, or even the classic Great Depression that hit, virtually, the entire world when the U.S. stock market crashed. More close to home would be the recession of 2008, or even the global economy's tumble due to the COVID-19 pandemic.

Cash isn't solid. It's liquid, yes, just as they say—but what they forget to tell you is that liquid can *evaporate*.

Unlocking Value

Moving, establishing, exchanging, and expanding value. Those are our areas of expertise at Idoneus. We have created, defined, and reimagined a new plane of value trading, and as such, have become a supplier of completely new forms of value for HNWIs and companies globally. We exist to help people and families like the family in the introduction find a way to trade their unneeded assets, protect their value, and find joy and security in this life, because they—and you, and all of us—deserve it. We achieve this through the trading of assets where new technologies are applied to mitigate risk and increase efficiencies and benefits for all parties.

I often like to say that Marco Polo began what we know as modern-day asset trading, but we intend to finish it.

Let's look at the problem objectively: there is trapped value in assets, whatever those assets may be. This is often (seemingly) true, and it may relate to your very situation. We can become your skeleton key; we can provide solutions to "unlock" your value and put it to work in another way, a way that will help you achieve your goals and access true freedom, all while maintaining a high level of security. We have built a platform with no barriers, and no borders, so that no matter where you are and no matter what is happening in any single locale you can immediately access your value and move it swiftly to where it is needed most.

I want to share a story with you that illustrates this point about the importance of being able to unlock value when needed. I had a client of a more senior age with a beautiful villa in a fairly desirable location in central Europe. The property was on a large parcel of majestic land. I was asked to come and meet her at the villa, which upon arrival seemed right out of a storybook, situated on the hilltop of a very significant private estate. Actually, I was already in Europe when she called me up, because I was dealing with a trade I told you about earlier—the 60-million-dollar trade involving the client with the huge ego who ended up blowing it all up for us. I like to make trips across the pond well worth my time. So we typically stack up opportunities when we are in the region and try to meet multiple clients—you're there for one transaction, but you capitalize on what's close. So while I was over there, I was happy to meet up with this potential new client in her gorgeous villa.

I drove out into the countryside where she was located—almost three hours from the airport—and arrived at a long driveway, after which I was greeted by this wonderful villa on the hillside in the distance. It was truly beautiful, huge, and above all, timelessly elegant. It was literally like a movie scene—there was a huge lake with swans swimming in it, and then the most dramatic stone villa you have ever seen against the backdrop of dense green forest. I could practically hear an orchestrated soundtrack as I came up the drive.

I pulled in front of the door in my Mercedes sedan, and the driver let me out. This woman opened the door—she was probably 74 years old, there by herself living in this huge villa. She explained to me that she had bought it probably eight or nine years previously as a gift for her husband, who was no longer there (for a lot of unique reasons). Now, she was managing this huge estate all by herself. She had renovated it with several million euros just in renovation costs after purchasing it.

She invited me inside the property. We sat by the fire, and she poured me some tea as we began to talk. She told me she found the property to be beautiful, as I did, but just couldn't manage it any longer and really wanted to find a buyer. She was referred to me, she said, when she began looking to sell (another example of my network coming through for me). A friend of hers—a client of mine—had told her that my company was *the* place to go if she needed to divest of the property privately and swiftly. If you don't have one of these assets, if you are not a member of the higher end, luxurious lifestyle, this might sound strange—but really, these properties are not easy to care for and even harder to sell, as anyone who owns one will tell you. There's a reason there are more people looking to sell than there are looking to buy. Getting stuck with an expensive property like this is more common than you might think, and this woman of more senior age was not willing to get stuck with something like this for, potentially, the rest of her life.

We talked until two in the morning about life, her business that she built, how she came to be where she is, and the assets that she owns. She was very, very intelligent, and this intelligence served her well—she spent all this time just getting to know me without discussing trade details so she could decide whether or not she could trust me about the business that she wanted to talk about.

After our long chat, she showed me to one of her 15 guest bedrooms and I settled in for the night. The next day, after breakfast, she showed me the grounds and the property, wowing me again and again, room after room. Afterward, we went to sit down and talk about business. She asked me, then, if I would please leave my cell phone outside in the hall. I did this, of course, but found it a bit strange. This was something I had never been asked to do before, except when dealing with royal families (while she was certainly wealthy, and had been a public figure, she wasn't royalty). She said, "I hope you don't mind, but I want to keep this very private and these phones are not private." No argument there. I left my phone in the hall, and she closed the door behind us.

She began to speak about the trust, the trust that owned the property, the trust that prefers this and doesn't prefer that, the trust that makes this decision and that decision. She kept talking about the trust in the third person, even though she was clearly the beneficial party of the trust. The "trust," she tells me, has decided they would like to liquidate.

She then began to speak about the trust's needs: to move out of the asset and to do it very, very discreetly, again reminding me of the royalty I had worked with. She didn't want to be on the market publically, since she had been a public figure recently and the acquisition itself had been very public. With so much of her life under the limelight, she was looking to make this very private in contrast. She indicated that she was open to trade for real estate and other assets around the world—real estate and assets that, while beautiful as well, wouldn't trap her or require quite so much work and effort as the one she was in currently. Properties and assets, she stressed, that were safe, secure, and above all, *private.*

This was the first time I had ever had a client with such a focus on privacy and discretion at that level. Other than working with a royal family member—when I experienced a similar situation—I have never seen someone ask me to remove my cell phone from the room for a simple discussion. Forget royalty—this was like working with a secret agent, or someone in witness protection! But we get all kinds of particular and peculiar requests, and I wasn't going to let her worries about privacy get in the way of our working together. After all, with a client base made up of successful entrepreneurs, celebrities, politicians, and some of the richest of the rich, this sort of thing is to be expected—though even so, the degree was a bit surprising.

The good news was, in her case, with a debt-free asset, she was very open to trade. As we got into it, what we really discovered was that she was in a cash pinch. The truth began to come out, slowly but surely. She didn't need or want another asset—she needed cash. Badly. She had found herself in a bit of an unsafe situation—let's leave it at that. As I've said, cash isn't king. Cash is *only* king if you don't have any, and, turns out, despite living in a property that would put a princess to shame, she didn't have any cash at this point in time. If you don't have cash, you need some, and that was her situation. She really wanted some cash liquidity, and while that's not usually our goal in a trade, I adored this lady—I thought she was fantastic, so I really wanted to help her.

Then she took the discussion in a direction I hadn't anticipated. With a smile on her face, over a beautiful lunch on the garden terrace, she offered me a chance to become a 50 percent owner of the property with no capital investment, not investing a dollar. She simply said, "I know you can help me. Would you become a partner with me on this, and help me do something with this property that I can't do?" She revealed that she wanted, it turns out, a huge development with more investment and improvements, supposedly making it a more attractive property for a trade or sale at a value multiple times the current market price. I tried to talk her out of it. I tried to explain—using my wisdom and expertise—why this wasn't the good idea it sounded like (the property was going to be a hard enough trade to begin with—adding even more value would just put it even further out of reach in this specific case), but she and her magical "trust" weren't agreeing, no matter which way I put it. It was breaking my heart, hearing her so set on something I knew wasn't going to bring in the return she was hoping for. I contemplated the situation for a number of weeks and spoke with her many times. But the more time went by, the more complicated the suggested plan became and was simply not feasible with her in her situation. I wanted to help her, but I wanted to *help* her, not jump with her from one sinking ship to another.

We ended up not transacting because I told her, "No, I don't want to go in on this property to develop it with you. I don't think that's what you need to be doing—you shouldn't be investing further into this property that you've already put so many millions of dollars into. You're likely not going to get the value out."

Unfortunately, she really should have traded, not improved the property and waited for someone to buy the property in cash—despite her need for cash. I could have traded her into multiple assets, diversified, and then she far more easily could have sold four or five smaller, lesser valued assets. That would have been much easier than trying to sell just one massive asset that was getting more massive all the time, but she just didn't agree to proceed, and no matter what I did, I couldn't convince her to do so. This was nearly 10 years ago. Last we communicated, she still owned the asset. I don't know how she managed to get through her situation without the cash she needed, but I can tell you this: it couldn't have been easy. That's the kind of stress no one should be dealing with on their own, never mind a woman in her 70s with little experience in the asset class, trying to get out of a tough situation with the world's tabloids watching her with a magnifying glass.

She's a total sweetheart, but I'll tell you this: I'm not going anywhere near that asset, no matter what! She's likely in an even tougher position today than she was then. This may not be a feel-good story, but it's the truth of what can happen. Even if you aren't airlifted out of a civil war like that first family, you can get stuck in an asset you don't want, needing cash you can't find because it is buried in an asset you can't sell. You can be making what seems like the best decision available to you, and it can all blow up in your face, depleting your bank accounts. People who built themselves up from a working-class background can suddenly find themselves treading water, somehow millions of dollars richer in net worth but in a tougher financial position than they were when they were flipping burgers during their time in university.

And yes—before you think this couldn't happen to you since you have so much value, or because you're "good with money" and know what you're doing, think again. Net worth means nothing if you can't unlock it and deploy it to where you need it to be, when you need it most. This isn't just about those extreme safety cases of wartime and rebellion, or people who make big mistakes, or people who do things in a less-than-proper way. The struggle to unlock value happens every day to people just like you, whoever you are, whatever your situation may be. It happens to people in peaceful or wealthy countries and to people in dangerous or poor countries, to people who have never financially struggled before and to people who deal with this kind of struggle daily. While the average person would never believe it, some people own islands worth a quarter of a billion dollars (or more) but are unhappy and highly stressed, because while they have a dream island, yes, they are completely unable to enjoy the money they earned and the assets they bought due to one reason or another—typically, trapped value.

I know of one very high-profile individual who owns such an island, a beautiful island that most people would think would be the perfect dream. If you don't have a private island, or have never experienced one, you might imagine something out of a cruise commercial—all palm trees and cocktails, hammocks, and sunsets. Who can be unhappy when they own their own private island? Well . . . this person is. Very unhappy, in fact—it's an open secret, in my circles, how much this person has grown to loathe their island. Upkeeping the island was more expensive than they anticipated, to the point that they had to come out of retirement and continue to work at an advanced age, just to pay the running costs. Can you imagine being so successful that you can buy an island worth well over $100 million, but then having to go back to work like you are in the struggling class because you suddenly can't pay the bills otherwise? Working paycheck to paycheck as a famous personality, financially back to square one? This sounds like a nightmare to me, and, I'm sure, to you.

Someone who does not understand the nuance of such situations might ask, "Why doesn't he just sell the island?"

Someone who does understand would probably reply, "It's not that simple." There aren't exactly long lines of people in the "private island" market at that price. Even I would have trouble sourcing a buyer for that island at the value they are seeking, admittedly—so is it hopeless?

Absolutely not.

Well, you may ask: what's the solution, then? Let me show you.

Enter: Idoneus

I am currently the Chief Executive Officer of Idoneus, a modern-day venture based on an ancient business model.

Idoneus is a company that facilitates high-value asset exchange by utilizing blockchain technology and a globally scalable platform to skip over the middleman (cash) and increase the security, speed, and transparency of the trading process. If this already sounds scary, just bear with me—I will explain, and quell all your fears.

"Blockchain" is a buzzword you may have heard lately and dismissed as a fad, but those who have studied the world of blockchain understand that it's strong, it's credible, and it's not going anywhere anytime soon. The most famous use of blockchain is probably Bitcoin, the digital currency that has been steadily picking up in popularity (and notoriety) in recent years. If you don't know anything about blockchain, you've still probably heard of Bitcoin. In simple terms, blockchain technology is an immutable database that is able to accurately track transactions without being tied to any central organization, government-issued fiat, or bank. Because it is not backed by a government (or any tangible commodity like gold or silver), Bitcoin is more mobile and is not controlled by any single entity. No government can decide to issue more Bitcoin;

no one person can easily cause Bitcoin to inflate or gain or lose value. It is completely its own entity, which makes a lot of people around the world very interested in it as a concept. There is, of course, risk to Bitcoin and other cryptocurrencies as an investment—as there is in any investment—but it is not nearly as scary as some people seem to think, and blockchain technology itself has many more applications than most people seem to understand—which is where our focus lies.

Blockchain technology is far more important than its initial application through Bitcoin. You may have also heard of the sudden growth of nonfungible tokens—or NFTs, for short—which also use blockchain in a similar way to grow and store digital value. There has even been talk of using the tracking features of blockchain to create secure digital voting to prevent voter fraud. Some are rolling their eyes at these innovations—these people remind me of those back in the early '90s who thought the internet was a waste of time, a flash in the pan. Far from a fad or a trend, blockchain is the future of high-value transactions—and if you plan to be a successful part of that future, I would sincerely suggest you begin learning as much as possible about blockchain technology before you're left behind, sending letters by courier in a digital world.

The possibilities of blockchain are truly endless, and that certainly hasn't escaped me. With the knowledge I have gained of blockchain in mind, I, along with some truly talented and intelligent associates, created Idoneus, a company with the express purpose of leveraging this new technology and putting it to work in my specialty arena of value exchange.

Let's use that individual with the massive private island as an example. They can't find a buyer for their island, so they come to me for help. Now, I could just leave them on the line while our team hunts around for a buyer or direct trade match, but that could take years (less time than it would take them to do it on their own, for sure—but still, a few years for such a transaction to go through is not uncommon). Selling or trading a unique and valuable asset like that in the traditional manner takes time, and can be very expensive. The owner would have to navigate several tasks before possibly getting to an agreeable cash exchange. After negotiating on price, marketing, travel costs, and appraisal opinions, they may finally receive an offer that is acceptable—but this is years in the future for most. All the while, throughout this process, the asset is very likely leaking value due to operating costs, inflation, changes in geopolitical risk, and other factors that can significantly impact the value of such a property. All the while, the owner is working every day to generate income, or in other cases pulling valuable liquidity from other sources to pay the very significant costs, and losing their time, money, and their patience. For centuries, that used to be the only way to transact with such an asset, but today, there is a completely new way to unlock value and monetize dormant equity that is trapped in unique physical assets of nearly all kinds.

Alternatively, instead of the traditional methods of sale or direct trade, we now have the ability to move value from an island, as in this example, into a specialized cryptocurrency such as IDON, which was designed specifically to facilitate such transactions.

What is IDON? IDON is a globally deployable, highly regulated digital currency that was created by Idoneus, a company based in Switzerland that has designed and built a platform to facilitate high-value exchange of assets, goods, and services for qualified high-net-worth individuals. IDON is like Bitcoin in that it is a cryptocurrency that utilizes blockchain, but unlike Bitcoin (which can be used by anyone and is traded on exchanges publicly by speculators), today IDON is only offered to qualified individuals and companies who are high-net-worth clients of Idoneus directly or private parties that qualified Idoneus clients decide to directly transact with. Essentially, Idoneus has created an exclusive, digital economy solely for the purpose of high-value asset trading. Our team has curated a large stable of assets in the portfolio today for trade—fine jewelry, rare art, timepieces, exotic vehicles, signature mansions, superyachts, islands, etc. If it is a well-known luxury asset category, we have probably traded it, or we have it coming into the portfolio very soon, along with high-net-worth trade partners from around the world who are fully KYC/AML checked and ready to transact. In our earlier example of the island owner, as long as the owner and the asset qualifies, the owner is now able to onboard their island into the Idoneus portfolio, and complete a transaction in short order. At the time of closing, the owner will receive full value in the Swiss payment token (IDON). No extensive red tape, no more holding costs, no more employee management or other asset management worries, just a straightforward transaction. They are now able to use their IDON as payment toward the purchase of other assets in (and out) of the Idoneus portfolio—properties, fine jewels, diamonds, a yacht, whatever they desire that comes available through the growing portfolio. Therefore, while not a direct exchange, they are making a trade with another of our clients indirectly, removing the need to meet and negotiate and instead just get down to the heart of it: trading value for value.

If the owner were to choose this path, they could trade out of the island nearly immediately, and at their discretion could exchange their new IDON holdings for an asset(s) that is something they actually could enjoy—or something with lower costs to maintain it and, therefore, less of a need to generate income to cover costs. Essentially, they will have traded their island for their retirement (or, perhaps, a beautiful home in Spain with one quarter of the maintenance and carry costs). They'll now have more of what is perhaps the most valuable asset of all, time for themselves, to spend with their families and enjoy their life, all thanks to the modern revolution of trade that Idoneus has brought to the marketplace.

And best of all, the parties involved do not have to be trading at the same time. Timing is everything, in traditional trade, but with IDON, a person who is trading an island this year can use their IDON to trade for a yacht that enters our portfolio next year, instead of only being able to trade for whatever happens to be available at the very same moment they complete their initial transaction. This ability to keep things "tradable" for years after they were traded for IDON allows for greater flexibility than ever before without the need to move out of physical assets into devaluing cash currencies in the interim. Ironically, not having to worry about time makes trades happen much faster!

This new borderless economy is not only for individuals, families, and companies. We see limitless applications to expand value. For example, there are countries that have valuable gold reserves in the ground but can't feed their people. There is now an opportunity to (nearly instantly) trade portions of their gold reserves through IDON for sustainable farmland owned by other parties around the world. In many cases, though, there is still too much red tape, too many unnecessary roadblocks in the way. The team at Idoneus is working to remove these barriers, for countries, for companies, for entrepreneurs, for you, for everyone. That is why Idoneus was founded. That is why IDON was created.

Imagine for a moment that you could take all the value you own that is trapped in dormant assets and put it to work for you, put it to work creating even more value for you that meets precisely the needs and goals you have. Imagine what you could achieve. Really—picture it, and take your time imagining this vision, because I'll tell you what it looks like: your perfect dream. For many, there is little that is more satisfying than looking back on a life well lived to see your major goals achieved, your family healthy and prospering, and an impressive collection of meaningful assets acquired, marking your successes along the way. But there is almost nothing more frustrating than spending half a lifetime to build your wealth and holdings to impressive levels, only to realize that you would pay almost anything to be given freedom from the responsibilities and burdens such wealth can bring. For decades, I have walked alongside valued clients and have seen up close the stress and difficulties this challenge can bring, and it is exactly why Idoneus was created—to introduce solutions to the market that change the game entirely.

If you're still on the fence, allow me to share with you just a few of our success stories. Of course, I can't go into full detail on them—I have to keep some of my trade secrets, after all! But I can tell you some exciting news that just might tip the scales for you here.

Recently, Idoneus actually facilitated the first trade of an original Pablo Picasso artwork. Not *our* first trade—*the* first documented Picasso trade via cryptocurrency that has ever been completed in the history of the world. It was a piece that had originally been purchased from the Marina Picasso collection, which was then traded for IDON. That was pretty major—it garnered a lot of media, a lot of news. To have a master's work—which is actually right here, in my office, as I write these words—trading in IDON was a big moment for Idoneus and the industry as a whole. It brought a lot of other collectors with artwork, other old masters' works, and many other collectors. A chain of people lined up—actually, we have a trade being negotiated right now for art valued at nearly $100 million (three paintings) that recently onboarded to transact through Idoneus. Much of this resulted from the Picasso transaction, and the excitement that generated about the ability to move value through Idoneus and blockchain technology. Many find it to be a very fitting, creative, groundbreaking way of trade for a master's painting and groundbreaking artists alike.

We are also negotiating and finalizing right now—by the time you have this book in your hands, it will have been completed—the trade of a very significant newly built superyacht where millions of dollars in IDON are being accepted. This is an important transaction because it is an indicator to the entire world of the quality and significance of assets that can be acquired and commissioned through the Idoneus platform. In this case, our client had been the owner of multiple properties in multiple countries in Latin America, some that he had been trying to sell for a number of years. Ten years earlier, they were part of an active plan to develop hotels and residential communities, but over time, our client had refocused his attention to his main business, and these properties and projects were no longer serving him. In this case, the client was able to facilitate an exchange for IDON, and then in the following 12 months he redeployed a portion of his equity into the build of his next superyacht where the shipyard accepted IDON toward his purchase. Truly extraordinary, especially considering the difficulty of monetizing properties like those he owned, as it can very easily take years to even find one interested buyer, never mind complete the sale for multiple seven-figure properties in such markets. If you don't have the right network, it's next to impossible. Thanks to Idoneus, we have the network and the technology to make transactions like this happen, and fast. Such transactions can be completed in days from the time of contract for service, not years, as was typical before Idoneus entered the marketplace. This superyacht transaction will make some very big news, so keep your eyes peeled for the stories.

We have focused significantly on real estate in the first few years since the company's inception, since that's where we had a lot of experience. We tended to focus on properties between $2 million and $10 million, because our team had many clients in that value range—it was where my team and I had the greatest experience. But now, as Idoneus develops and expands, what we're focused on probably more than anything is bringing in more options for utility for token holders. Now in addition to high-value assets, we're actively creating partnerships to bring additional luxury items, goods, and services with lower values because our clients are seeking items of value from $20,000 to $1 million just as much as they are decamillion-dollar trades.

As mentioned earlier, we are actively negotiating the onboarding and trade of gold reserves and even operating gold mines for IDON. The idea of a gold-mine acquisition for Idoneus is very compelling, because it opens many doors of trade that our focus on real estate had previously kept firmly closed. As time went on with Idoneus, we realized that we (and our clients) would much rather have a gold production company that onboards $30 million in gold or fine jewels on the platform (priced from $50,000 to $350,000) than have three properties worth a collective $30 million (at $10 million a piece). That's the real value of a partnership with a producing gold mine, and the reason we've onboarded some of the most valuable jewels in the world, such as extraordinarily rare Burma rubies, Muzo emeralds, and GIA-certified diamonds. We are very focused on constant growth of the IDON utility available for our clients, in order to continue to see growth in the global transaction velocity of IDON as well.

While I lead a team that is very skilled and focused to facilitate decamillion-dollar value exchanges, we are just as focused today on bringing in lower value—but still luxury—assets, goods, and services that will more easily facilitate beneficial trades for our clients and allow them to diversify out of their single-asset, substantial holdings. Partnerships with companies, be it jet companies, yacht charter companies, luxury retailers, fine jewelers, diamond dealers, companies that sell gold coins and gold bars—we have team members and asset advisors working around the clock on five continents to create valuable partnerships with industry leaders and companies invested in these areas and work with them to discover ways that they will benefit from accepting IDON as a preferred method of payment. This will allow them to trade their current assets, goods, and services inventory indirectly for real estate, many other substantial physical assets, or valuable goods and services. Really, no matter who you are, if you are a qualified owner, company, or facilitator in the luxury sector, Idoneus was created to help you reach your goals.

All that said, even if you don't currently want to trade your multimillion-dollar properties, you can still benefit greatly from being involved with Idoneus. We offer many options for people seeking to divest—of everything from more volatile cryptocurrency to devalued fiat currency to a collection of Rolex watches, an exquisite diamond, or even your 42-foot Sea Ray cruiser yacht or Lamborghini Aventador—if you have an extra on hand. Not everything must be in the millions to be desirable to our high-net-worth clients. Even if you have no assets you wish to sell or trade today, but are interested in being a part of the future of value and being in a position to benefit from the economy we are building together, we can help!

We have had clients trade their assets for IDON, and at times, those physical assets have lost value due to many factors, but they did not experience that value loss and instead have at times gained value, since the collective Idoneus economy and IDON utility itself continued to grow during the same period. There are clients who not long ago traded assets for IDON and now enjoy buying power to purchase significantly more value than their previous asset value with the IDON they earned from a single transaction. Take all this on top of the hundreds of millions of dollars in properties, art, gemstones, vehicles, yachts, etc., which are available through Idoneus today, and there's simply no denying that IDON and Idoneus are not just the future of trade, but the present of trade as well. The future of high-value transactions has been changed forever through advances in technology and process introduced by Idoneus. If you are a qualified participant, I welcome you to consider joining us.

And yes, I'm also talking to you crypto natives, you who made a digital fortune early on in the space. I know many of you are longtime HODLers, though may be growing weary of the volatility of Bitcoin and other cryptocurrencies and are now seeking to move into a less volatile, but still digital, model that is asset-centric. We've welcomed many of you into the IDON economy already, and I anticipate many more are soon to follow—especially with Bitcoin's recent performance. What's perhaps most attractive about IDON is that participants enjoy many of the benefits that drew you into cryptocurrency initially, but unlike currencies like Bitcoin, IDON also enjoys real utility from the start. Almost no one who invested in Bitcoin, or ETH, etc., really early wants to go to cash with all their holdings today—most are far too savvy for that. Instead, in most cases what they are asking for is to lateralize a portion of their holdings into physical assets of significance as a hedge against the volatility of their other holdings, and there are very few groups who can actually facilitate that today. Idoneus can! If this message connects with you, well, you know who to call.

The IDON Revolution

What Jeff Bezos has done for retail with Amazon, we intend to do for asset trading via Idoneus. Redefining and redesigning, revolutionizing the field and bringing it into the 21st century—and beyond. Our focus is to help our clients preserve their wealth, while understanding that in many cases they may not want their wealth in the same form as it is right now. Hence, asset trading—keeping the wealth intact, while the form of value shifts quickly, efficiently, and securely. We focus every effort to provide avenues to help our clients' value stay steady, or grow, even while the thing that holds the value changes (from "fine art" to IDON to "commercial real estate" to "acres of producing farmland" to "diamonds" and back again as the client desires).

Asset trading is a challenging career, but also a rewarding one—and while it's complicated, it's also, in its own beautiful way, elegantly simple. People often acquire things they think they want, but soon realize they don't need. People then discover they actually require a lot less than they thought they did. When they reach this point and realize they have acquired assets they no longer want but perhaps cannot quickly sell via typical paths, I help them re-achieve equilibrium and peace in their lives by trading those assets for value that actually leads them to what they truly want, all with special attention to keep their overall wealth and value more or less at the same level during the process. By using IDON, the stress of a traditional trade is eliminated—the need to trade right now or risk losing the ability to trade this asset for months or years while we wait for the perfect transaction partner is completely erased. It's as simple as that, made complicated by the world we live in, made simple again by Idoneus.

Like Bezos, we are taking something that already exists—in his case, online shopping; in our case, blockchain—and making it work for us in a slightly different way—in his case, to sell books (and eventually, everything); in our case, to trade the world's most unique and beautiful forms of physical value. IDON, like Bitcoin, is digital, but unlike Bitcoin, which is not backed by anything but public opinion, IDON is part of a highly asset-centric ecosystem. This does not mean that each IDON is asset-backed directly (it is not), but because of the design of the private, closed-loop business model and the function of the token itself, as well as the utility that the Idoneus platform offers, it does mean that IDON holders are much less likely to see plummeting pricing of IDON, like what has happened with Bitcoin and many other digital currencies that have no access to tangible assets nor any real-world utility built into their models. Idoneus has utilized smart contract technology and designed the currency from the beginning to ensure the greatest level of stability for all participants. Therefore, it operates more as a type of hedge than the completely speculative, free-floating, market-making, influenced Bitcoin where the opinion of the "mob" on any day can swing values by double digits. While there is risk—as there is in anything—risk is mitigated substantially by the IDON design and function itself. Idoneus clients range from the most conservative risk-averse type to the type who find skydiving a little tame, but all of them have one thing in common. They each understand value. They also know that value is very personal and comes in many forms. IDON is merely the latest evolution of value, which has been evolving for thousands of years.

IDON has allowed many to speed up the process of asset trading and sale, making it more efficient and easy to complete beneficial transactions. If your assets are no longer working for you, you do *not* need to keep them on your balance sheet— no matter how challenging it might seem, and no matter how significant those assets are, you do not need to keep them and should not keep them if they are not meeting your needs and are draining valuable resources, financial or otherwise. You *can* trade them now—in most cases, almost immediately.

Moral of the story: don't just sit on your assets until something truly irreversible occurs. If you don't want them any longer, trade them and redeploy your value in a manner that meets your needs and future goals. It is possible—I and the Idoneus team are working to do so every day, with clients in similar situations around the globe. We can help you, and we can help you in a way that avoids having to go through incredibly slow and complicated cash transactions that in many cases simply increase your costs, risks, and frustration. As we have discussed already, staying traditional while navigating nontraditional market conditions will typically result in the loss of value in the long run, even if only due to devaluation from overexposure, inflation, and ownership costs. Instead, we will utilize IDON through Idoneus, linking you into a fully KYC'd community of like-minded, high-net-worth individuals where you can free up your personal value mobility in a way that meets your requirements for security and comfort as you look into the future.

In Summary

The exchange of value is certainly a primary part of our business, but another significant aspect is following what actually holds value. The value of everything changes over time—that's why we must be wary of inflation, intentional and even unintentional manipulation of markets, as we consider the acceptance of any currency for truly unique and valuable assets. Through Idoneus, we have delivered a solution to the market that can assist clients around the world to achieve their goals quickly and securely, in a more beneficial manner than was ever possible before.

Not only do the value of assets quite literally change over time, but so does the mindset and priorities of individuals. Every human's personal view of value changes over the course of their lives. That which you valued in your 20s may not be on your list in your 50s, 60s, 70s, or beyond, but the future—even of your own values and preferences—is impossible to predict, so flexibility ("asset mobility") is of primary importance to consider at all times. Now that we are aware of the ability to transfer value nearly on demand, let's move on and discuss the evolution of value on a personal level, and how I can help you achieve more peace of mind during this process no matter how many candles are on your birthday cake.

Chapter Six

Evolving Value

"Things do not change; we change."
—Henry David Thoreau

Here's another question for you to ponder with me: if you had to choose between $100,000 in cash, or $100,000 in travel, no strings attached, which would you choose? There's no wrong answer, so be honest.

Generally, if you chose the $100,000 in travel, I would guess that you belong to one of the younger generations, and if you chose the $100,000 in cash, I would guess that you belong to the more senior generations.

Was I right?

Value is evolving, every day, on a micro and macro scale. On a macro scale, things like BTC, NFTs, blockchain, and other technologies are changing the way value is expressed and exchanged, as we already learned in the last chapter. We are doing the same thing, as you now know, with IDON.

Our clients at Idoneus are less concerned about growing value extraordinarily; they are far more concerned about losing value than they are about creating more of it. The stock market soaring to its highest level doesn't really excite them—market conditions that might indicate that a historic *crash* is imminent would draw much more attention—which is why we have worked to put a system in place to protect value above all.

Just as the market can change the value of the dollar, the value of assets can change, too—and I'm not just talking about deterioration or inflation. There are certain assets that are more valuable today to our culture than they were yesterday. For example, natural resources are now rarer, and therefore more valuable. In years past, it was hardly noticed when a company cut down a forest to make furniture, since furniture was seen by many as more valuable than forests in their natural form. Today, people generally greatly care if you cut down a forest in order to manufacture a product of any kind, since forests are rarer and therefore viewed as more valuable.

On the other hand, other things that used to hold value are now less valuable. Coal mines were once a very valuable asset and business, but today they are a far riskier investment with much less market support. While it used to be a great way to gain wealth, now you could face protests, vandalism, limitations, or even shutdowns by governments. I once spent more than 500 days working on the trade of a substantial coal reserve that was part of a very significant development and manufacturing project. I certainly learned a lot about coal and the process to monetize it, but I can candidly say that I would not invest even one day on such an asset today. Value changes, and it changes quickly. A more classic example is the old saying about how a new car loses much of its value the moment it is driven off the lot.

Let's look deeper at that $100,000 question I posed to you at the beginning of this chapter. As I explained, in my experience, I'd say it is more likely for people in the younger generations to typically prefer the $100,000 in travel option because those younger people in those generations are more likely to value experiences over material goods. That is a reflection in a shift in the overall Western culture. They would choose the travel option, more often than not, because that is what they would probably spend the money on anyway. They are the ones giving vacations to each other rather than physical objects on birthdays; they are the ones saving up for a ziplining excursion in Costa Rica at their residential membership club rather than a permanent summer home. They are less likely than the older generation to want to buy and own things like mansions or yachts. They are *more* likely to want to rent them for a week, to enjoy all the benefits of an asset like this without any of the downsides—namely, the costs of upkeep, taxes, and the hassle of selling or trading it later. This is actually where the market as a whole is going—look no further than the exploding popularity of Airbnb for proof of that. Young people don't want to own a vacation home; they want to rent one for a weekend, then rent a different one in a different location next year, and another one the year after that.

The older generations may find this to be ludicrous, but it's all a matter of perspective and what you value. Put judgment aside, wherever you are on the age spectrum, and focus instead on acceptance: no matter what you do, a younger person may never be interested in buying a vacation home in Barbuda. So, how does the world of high-value assets have to adjust to suit the changing demographics and changing values? Well, it's more complicated than you might think, because we're not just talking about generational differences. Your own values also will change over your life—more than once.

Personal Value Evolution

Values change over an individual's lifespan—no exception. I have seen clients who have spent 20, 30, 40 years working to achieve the mega-rich, superyacht lifestyle. They want the private jet, they want the mansion, they want the castle in the south of France—and then they get it. Then, a few years later, they call us to get rid of it—to get rid of the jet, the mansion, the castle, the yacht—because after a little time has passed, they have realized in many cases that they actually want anything *but* that.

If you have children like I do, you have probably experienced this on a micro scale. I imagine all the parents out there reading this book are laughing to themselves, thinking about the trumpet or ballet shoes or hockey equipment you paid for only for it to sit in a closet after the child got bored of it and moved on. The appeal wore off, and, believe it or not, the same thing can happen to adults and *their* "toys," too—even if those toys cost millions of dollars. The only difference is that you can't just shove a 200-acre estate in Spain into your attic and forget about it, especially not when it holds 15 percent of your net worth.

I've had clients who, though not a decade before were dying to buy a triple-deck superyacht, came to me more than willing to trade that very yacht for farmland in Colorado. Why? Because they realized real value, to them, was not where they thought it was—or, alternatively, their values shifted over time to something they never would have thought they would have wanted previously. This example is actually a true story. I found a rancher out west who had ranches in multiple states who agreed to trade one of those ranches for a superyacht. He didn't necessarily want a superyacht, but he was looking for a change in his life, and this was a great way to do it. Fortunately, the owner of one of the superyachts we represented was done with that lifestyle and wanted to acquire more land. He was looking for a life change, to live more simply and quietly, as he said it. He also understood well that land with water rights, land in that part of the world, was going to go up in value while his yacht was going down in value, making it a great trade in his perspective. I sat down with the clients, facilitated the trade, and they both walked away happy with their new asset—they both traded something they used to value for something they valued more, now.

That was more than 10 years ago. At the time, each of the assets were of very similar value. I would say that the ranch, today, is worth approximately three times what the yacht is worth. And they agreed to trade even. So you really have to know where you want to be, what your goals are, and what is personally valuable to you.

That's not to say the person who owned several ranches and traded one for the yacht made a bad decision, or that he regrets having made it today. He had land like the U.S. Treasury has dollar bills. Hundreds of thousands of acres of land. He wanted something new, and the other gentleman wanted anything but a superyacht. They both wanted to move out of the assets they currently had. Obviously, the yacht may have more avenues to liquidity with a global market of potential buyers, but it also has much more volatility in terms of value. It's a depreciating asset, as we've seen above. But the ranch owner wasn't necessarily looking for long-term value growth. He just wanted a yacht, some fun, something different. Buying a yacht is, obviously, not a very lucrative investment in most cases, but making more money wasn't his goal—his value—at the time of this trade. So we had an east-coast yacht owner flying out west to look at a ranch, and a rancher flying to the east coast to sit on the back of this superyacht cruising along the Miami skyline. We've seen every trade you can imagine in this business!

All that to say, the reason why this field is so unique is because of the great diversity of personalities and values in my clients. Everyone has different perspectives on value, and these differences can result in some interesting trades, which, nevertheless, result in both parties walking away very satisfied.

While on the subject, I can tell you today that yacht owners are some of my favorite clients. The wealthier people are, the more fickle and impatient they can be. When they are done with something, they are absolutely done, and never is that more true than with a person who owns a yacht. Yacht owners are typically highly confident, competent, and, at times, emotional people. You don't buy a superyacht unless emotions play a factor in your asset acquisition decisions. It's not based on finances or wisdom—you just want a yacht! You're doing it even though you are certain the asset will not make you money, nor increase your net worth. You're doing it because you want a superyacht—even though you know it's going to cost you millions of dollars to run a year. You know it's going to go down in value by even more millions of dollars over time. And you're still buying one! That's an emotional decision. And so long as you're well aware of that going into it and don't have any unreasonable expectations, that's all perfectly okay. We can make that happen. We can get you out of the asset you currently own and onto that yacht—and later, down the line, when you want your life to be more stable and less volatile, less "party in the Mediterranean" and more "mint juleps on the porch," we can trade you out of that yacht and into something you can grow old in—without multimillion-dollar refits and costly maintenance every 12 to 24 months. That's why I love these kinds of clients—they buy many different kinds of assets just because they want them, and they move them around like little matchbox cars in the backyard. They're fun to work with, plain and simple.

This is the mentality of these clients. They will trade a five-million-dollar property as fast as most people would trade a five-dollar bill. They just want out, and we are the way out. We are the safe, secure, regulated, legal way to move out of any asset that you no longer want to own and move into a new horizon, a new asset class. That's Idoneus.

I've had a lot of clients come to me as they realize their personal values are changing as they are growing older. They no longer want to spend their time worrying about making enough money to pay the holdings costs of their private chateau and winery, or managing repairs to three or four holiday homes. They no longer find joy in cruising into the marina in the biggest yacht in the harbor, or watching others' eyes gleam wide with envy when they check the time on their one-of-a-kind timepiece. It's no longer about the zeroes piling up in the bank account—it's rather about the candles adding up on the birthday cake, and the dwindling numbers of truly precious moments left in their life.

That's how you find people trading oceanfront mansions in the Bahamas for small lakefront houses in Lake Tahoe, or not even caring *what* we trade for as long as we get them out of the resource- and energy-draining asset they currently want to move on from. The biggest factor in trade is that people want *out* of what they have—whatever it is that they have, be it castles, superyachts, fine art, a collection of jewels, or even a ranch out west—and they want to move into something else of value that meets their new plans and needs. It's crazy, if you're not in this world, to think about—it sounds really simple, but that's the truth. People want out of what they have and they want to move into something that provides them with more options. Idoneus is a pathway to facilitate that trade very swiftly, since we no longer are required to make direct asset exchanges or traditional sales—and are able to utilize IDON instead.

We had a call with someone a couple weeks ago—this person is part of a very successful family, a very wealthy family. They own properties all over Central America. She heard I was in the area for another asset we were reviewing and asked if we would come down to check out one of her estate properties. It was only 40 minutes away from where I was, so I agreed and sent one of my closest associates down to see the property. The estate was truly impressive and just one of many properties they own. This family has land everywhere, almost too much land, and it was all across Central America, and she told us that they want to diversify. She said, without prompting, "By the way, we take crypto. We're very open to that." A phrase we are hearing more and more now from asset trading clients seeking new avenues to monetize their valuable assets. As I am writing these words to you, we are writing up the details for the trade of one of these properties. It's happening everywhere, and it's happening for them because they have 60 or 70 different properties in the market and they desire to divest of about 50 percent of them. They don't need cash; they need value. They don't need never-ending land assets either—what they need is something that gives them more options, more freedom, and can lead to something they will enjoy, something they personally value. This is what we deliver.

Similarly, I had a client from Mexico. She is very wealthy and has several properties she would like no longer to own. This was multigenerational, old money, traditional wealth we were dealing with. Not a new-money type of mentality. But we were able to meet with her and talk about value exchange and talk about how to move from one single physical asset to many other assets over time. In the midst of that discussion, while it wasn't the right time for her to trade her estate, we discovered that she had a very significant collection of heirloom jewelry she wanted to trade. We both agreed that it was a great way to test the water with this new technology and currency that she (like many others from her generation) was somewhat hesitant about. So, we created a trade where she could divest a few significant pieces that would help her step into this new digital economy in a way that was comfortable for her—much more comfortable than jumping into trading a 20,000-square-foot oceanfront property as her first step. Today she is far more comfortable with our process, and I will be surprised if we don't hear from her again in the near future about going forward with the property trade through the Idoneus platform.

On this note, I should mention that very rare fine jewelry is one of the asset classes we plan to expand even further into than we have in the past. So often, we see members of wealthy families inherit rare fine jewelry that they simply do not wish to own—it may be very valuable, but perhaps it is deemed to be out of fashion, or they have too many other pieces already—or simply do not know what to do with it. Through Idoneus, we can help transform these forms of value into a globally deployable currency, which can be used as payment toward the acquisition of assets, goods, and services of many kinds. Even better, we can make sure these jewels find a home with someone at fair retail value who will truly appreciate them, not just some shop trying to purchase from the family at the lowest possible value in order to sell for many times what they paid.

As we've learned, people who most often say, "Cash is king," are typically those who don't have any, and people who pursue the dream of owning a private island full-throttle likely have never owned one. The grass is always greener, after all, and sometimes, people (even the wealthiest people) get their values out of balance. All of us at some point may value achievement so much that we might undervalue relationships for a time. And others value their individual experiences so much they never make it home for the holidays with family. Before we know it, decades have gone by, children have grown, and a new phase of life begins. It is often during these times that my clients realize that a 10-bedroom beachfront villa or perfectly curated art collection has little value any longer if there is no one to share it with but themselves. Everything has a price, and everything has value, but as Warren Buffett rightly said, price is what you pay; value is what you get. We all must be vigilant to balance the price we pay in time, money, resources, and relationships with the value that we receive in return.

What you truly value gets your attention, time, focus, and commitment. This goes both ways. This was why I mentioned, earlier, that my team and I have learned to be cautious when people don't respect our time, always rescheduling, showing up late, leaving early, or even not showing up to our prearranged meeting at all. If they really valued us, you can be sure they would have been there on time. I'm willing to travel around the world for my clients; if they're not willing to reschedule a dentist appointment, or set an alarm so they get to our meeting on time, that speaks volumes to me about how much they value me (a one-time adjustment is one thing, but a repeated offense is a clear indicator of where their values really lie). In business, we value our clients, and we show that through our punctuality and respect.

As a person reaches certain milestones in their career and/or their life, their values change, and therefore what gets their attention, time, focus, and commitment changes. What they value most often becomes *time*. Time, as most people eventually realize, is *the* most valuable asset. People value time with their assets, time with their family, time doing what they love. Their values evolve, and they realize that time is the most important thing to them. This especially becomes true when it becomes more evident that time is running out.

I have never heard of anyone who, at the end of their life, said things like, "I wish I had one more platinum mine." No. They say, "I wish I had one more *year*." They would trade all their yachts and estates and jewels for one more year. One more year with their spouse, with their children, one more year on this Earth. Once our time is gone, that's it. There is not a single asset in any of our portfolios that can extend our time for even a moment.

What we value changes drastically at different cycles in life, and I get a front-row seat to that with some of my clients who are further along their journey than me. It's a sobering reminder that our most valuable assets truly are the precious moments we have to enjoy this life.

Shifting Values

There are so many different types of assets. Some are tangible, such as real estate, businesses, land, art, and so on, while others are more intangible and personal, like time, family, health, and relationships. What is an asset to one person may not be an asset to you, and vice versa. That is not necessarily a sign of another person being unwise, but rather just being *another person.*

The younger professional just starting out won't typically value their own time or relationships as much as a more established person. The younger person may at times ignore their family and stay late, working 14-,16-, or 18-hour days to climb the ladder of success. They might not focus on their health, mental or physical. For a period, they may not have a strong focus on relationships at all and might instead be laser focused on purchasing the home or business of their dreams— and they can make that happen. Many do, and we can help them achieve that.

And when that person ages, their values will almost certainly shift again. They may have no desire for another business, or another holiday home, or a Jackson Pollock painting; they might not find value in owning yet another diamond mine either. They will very often desire more time with their friends and family, more time doing what they love—more time. Less time managing their holiday homes, less time negotiating with a buyer for their carefully curated car collection, less time toiling away in their business only to send their hard-earned income to cover carry costs on assets they rarely enjoy anymore. This is how it's supposed to be—a natural maturing process that leads us all to where we find the greatest and most authentic forms of value. Shifting values is a sign of wisdom and experience, of having lived life well and now getting the opportunity to enjoy it, to reap the benefits, to do exactly what you want when you want to do it. We can help clients at this stage achieve their goals, too, just as we help younger clients in the building phase design a lifestyle of their dreams while navigating their current stage of the journey.

Shifting values is not a bad thing. There is no "right" or "wrong" thing when it comes to value, just as it is not "right" or "wrong" to prefer a holiday in the mountains over a holiday at the beach. Differences, both between us and others and between different versions of ourselves, are a natural consequence of the variety of life. And it is the reason why asset trading was invented by our ancient ancestors and still thrives today.

One man's trash is another man's treasure, and vice versa. And believe it or not, this holds true for assets from Ferraris to castles and everything in between.

I'm not telling you what to value, and I'm not implying any one thing is better than the other. In fact, just the opposite—I am expressing the simple truth that all these things *do* have value, even if they don't have value to you, and therefore, any of these things can be traded for one another and are every day. That is, if you have the knowledge, experience, and ability to see such a trade to completion.

At Idoneus, we have decades of experience doing exactly this and hundreds of years of collective experience on our team ready to serve you. My team and I can help you trade out of your operating diamond mine in South Africa into IDON and into a farm in Montana, or oceanfront estate in Nevis, or perhaps multiple other assets of your choice that meet your requirements. And the excess IDON liquidity you might receive in the same transaction could allow you to trade into other assets that can provide other sources of income over time without the need for direct oversight—and by doing such, may give you three, five, or even ten years of additional free time with your family to enjoy instead of operating your current holdings thousands of miles from where you truly desire to be. You can quite literally "buy time" with your current assets. You tell us what you are working toward and we'll take care of the transactional end of things; all you have to do is pay attention to, and understand, what you value.

What you *really* value, not just what society tells you to value.

In Summary

Pay close attention to your values shifting over time, and honor them. Don't assume that purchasing another villa, or another jet, or another yacht will make you happy. If you don't value it, if your priorities have already shifted, having it in your possession will not change your mind. In fact, depending on where your values are at the moment, such a decision may bring more anxiety than peace or joy.

We must also pay attention to the world and how it's changing, because the world is changing, whether we like it or not—and the world views on value are changing. Much of the world no longer values assets like coal mines as it once did. The younger generations no longer value material possessions as much, and that preference is going to shape the world to come. Yes, values are personal, but there are overarching trends in society that can, if studied, teach us what people are more or less likely to value in the future, based on their age and demographics. This knowledge serves us very well as we consider future investments.

Changing values is not a negative thing. It is a part of the development of humanity and always has been. The world evolves and changes; people evolve and change—that is how life works, and the explosion of information and technology that began a few decades ago and is continuing exponentially through to this day has been, and is, changing a lot of value points in the world very rapidly.

If you have questions about options that are available to you for a specific asset trade or simply wish to strategize about how to successfully manage your personal asset portfolio, we would be honored to assist you in navigating this tumultuous and ever-changing environment by sharing our experience and resources with you. The reality is that for many this is a scary time, but it doesn't have to be. All you have to do is reach out to us.

If your and my most valuable asset is time, the world's most valuable asset is nature. As our company moves into the future, we are focusing more on sustainability. This, like the evolution of value, is also effective on a micro and macro scale.

It is time we look into what preserving value looks like, both for you personally and for the planet we all share.

PART THREE

PROTECTING VALUE

Chapter Seven

Mobility and Personal Preservation

"Change before you have to."
—Jack Welch

Do you remember the first time you purchased something online? Do you remember holding your breath, maybe even backing out of the page when you were asked to type in your credit card information? Or maybe you remember feeling mildly surprised when the item you ordered actually showed up?

How far we've come. I was certainly nervous the first time I ordered something online. Now, like many of us, I have a package from Amazon and other online retailers on my doorstep nearly every day. The internet is now intrinsic to every waking moment of most of our lives. Can you remember the last full day you went without accessing the internet?

When the internet first started gaining popularity, a lot of people didn't see the point of the technology at all. Why would you ever need so-called "electronic mail"? Who would even use something like that, when we already have fax machines and answering machines? As time went on and the internet became more and more widely used, it shifted from something incomprehensibly high tech and seemingly pointless to the average user to something most people, it was clear, would soon be interacting with on a daily basis. That's when things started feeling scary—people became nervous of computer viruses, of hacking, of putting photos of themselves online. These fears were based in reality, of course—the early internet could be a scary place. But that changed, as time went on and the internet became more ubiquitous.

Today, the internet is so interwoven into our lives it can be strange and difficult, as I mentioned, for most of us to go more than a day or two without it—or even a few hours, or minutes, depending on your generation. We have all seen two- and three-year-olds work their way around an iPad with ease. While there are still risks to the online world, we understand those risks and have systems in place to mitigate them, making the internet much less of a scary and unfamiliar place.

I believe the same thing is happening with the rising blockchain technology, and soon, which is why we see so much focus on digitizing and tokenizing value through blockchain. Right now it may be something unfamiliar and strange, something your techy nephew tries to explain in vain on Thanksgiving, but before you know it, it will be a part of our everyday lives—just as much, perhaps, as the internet is right now. I believe this for many reasons, but if we only look at the rate of adoption of blockchain being applied globally, we can all see major change coming at a staggering pace.

A recent poll of industry leaders shows that the implementation of blockchain technology is viewed in a highly favorable light, with almost 90 percent of the businesses polled already utilizing blockchain technology in some capacity, and 87 percent intending on investing in blockchain within the next year. Here are a few statistics regarding blockchain and cryptocurrency to consider:

- Global spending on blockchain in 2021 reached $6.6 billion.
- Over 300 million people, 3.9 percent of the total world population, use blockchain for cryptocurrency.
- There are over 82 million Bitcoin wallets in existence.
- Companies are projected to spend almost $19 billion on blockchain technology in 2024.

Currently there is a stigma and a lack of understanding about blockchain. For example, it was revealed in that poll of industry decision-makers that 54 percent of them still see the terms "cryptocurrency" and "blockchain" as interchangeable, even though 73 percent felt confident in their understanding. In the very near future, blockchain—and the value delivered by platforms and companies leveraging it—will become clearer to the general public, causing an outbreak of adoption to the masses that will revolutionize several of the largest industries on the planet. If that surprises you, you may not be monitoring the trends as closely as we are. Blockchain technology has already forever changed the way value is exchanged, but soon we will see it accepted and used across the world as commonly as emails are sent today. The idea of buying a large mansion with fiat (cash) in many parts of the world will soon feel as outdated as buying it with a wagon full of tools crafted from obsidian stone, as our ancient ancestors would have proposed. Value is transforming again—as it always has. Don't miss it.

One of the other areas of change we see is the shift toward short-term experience exchange. As mentioned earlier, the younger generation doesn't seem interested in owning expensive yachts and mansions anymore, but they do want to rent them. Like any transaction, rentals can be tracked immutably on blockchain, and therefore, an asset's income history can be accounted for by the owner and proven to a future buyer at a level of certainty never seen before. As blockchain accounting becomes the standard instead of the exception, there will no longer be opportunities for unscrupulous asset owners to provide accounting reports that are not 100 percent accurate— something I have seen many times throughout my career. This is just another example of the application of the technology that my team is focused to develop for the benefit of every client. The focus on blockchain is about far more than just tracking value and accounting, however. Indeed, blockchain is a new tech highway offering qualified and savvy participants a new level of mobility that increases even our personal security.

Blockchain Security in a Dangerous World

People tend to think the worst will never happen to them, but it can, and if you are not prepared, it very likely will. If you don't have the ability to move at the first sign of danger, or at least have a plan in place to protect your assets, you can lose very significant wealth in a matter of weeks or even days. We've discussed this already, but if you're still not convinced, maybe this example will open your eyes to the reality of the situation.

Over a decade ago, I had a potential new client call me from Toronto asking if we could arrange an immediate trade of their mulimillion-dollar oceanfront estate in Mexico. He shared that he and his wife recently retired and that they were no longer using the property in Mexico and preferred to trade it for another asset in the U.S. or Canada. He was in his mid-60s. I could tell immediately that this was a very intelligent man, but I also sensed a uniquely high level of urgency in his voice. After a bit of discovery, we learned that his property was in great jeopardy. It had been taken over months earlier and was being occupied by a powerful local drug cartel. He had no access, no control, no way into his own house! Can you imagine?

I remember the discussion with the owner about our findings and can still hear the desperation in his voice, hoping that we could help him somehow. What options did the client have at that point? In reality, *none.* We learned that he had been trying to sell the asset through traditional channels for two years prior to the cartel noticing it was unoccupied and deciding to move into the beautiful beachfront compound six months earlier. He was told by the local small-town municipality that if he could arrange a sale they would go in and assist in getting the cartel to move out. I think we all know the chances of that strategy working out well. I had no options for him. I certainly wasn't about to facilitate the trade of this property to another valued client who would expect to be able to utilize it as intended. I pride myself in my ability to trade value of nearly any kind—but that kind of trick just isn't in my playbook. So, that potential new client was simply out of luck. They did too little, far too late. This is a simple example where with a proper plan in place we could have moved them out of the asset long before it was such a dangerous situation. Given only 30 days, today my team could have saved this gentleman from enduring millions of dollars in losses. Better yet, he might have avoided the entire experience altogether if he called us years earlier, as we would not have suggested an acquisition in that specific part of Mexico at that precise time.

Within one or two transactions, we can move a client and their family out of a precarious position *with* their value intact in a transparent, safe, and legal manner. We can help you move that three-million-dollar, 10-million-dollar, or even one-billion-dollar asset base of value very quickly when things get dangerous. And they can get dangerous, no matter who you are or where you reside—and this is increasingly true as time goes on, unfortunately.

You are probably already aware of the tense political environment that has allowed anti-rich sentiments to spread like wildfire around the globe. There is a growing belief, especially among young people, that the wealthy do not deserve the wealth and assets they have worked so hard to achieve. Fewer and fewer young people aspire to achieve high levels of monetary success because of this growing belief, and along with this lack of aspiration, there is a lack of honor toward the wealthy that goes along with it. Have you seen this in your own life? There is a lack of trust and respect of the upper classes and of capitalistic business in general, and you can see it in every strike, riot, and new union cropping up in your local coffee shop, every social media post about how "unfair" practically anything that has to do with a wealthy person is. Sure, most of it you can just ignore or write off as jealousy, as a misunderstanding of the truth—but there are times when these sentiments can turn dangerous, and even violent, and with the popularity of these thoughts spreading, this risk of danger grows by the minute. This is the modern danger of great success, and you can see it all over the world. From Beverly Hills, to Paris, to Rio de Janeiro. There are very few safe havens left.

A few years ago, I met a prospective client in a restaurant in Beverly Hills. Someone I was with pointed at his very expensive timepiece worth over $500,000 and told me that just last month, he had his watch stolen right off his wrist at gunpoint at the very place we were having lunch. I was shocked—not just that it happened there in broad daylight in Beverly Hills, but that he went out and bought another one so quickly. Not only that, but he felt comfortable wearing it—and in the same establishment where he was robbed! I remember the gentleman nodded knowingly, and told me that it was just a part of being alive right now. He went on to share his belief that one can't let fear control their life. He said, "What am I to do? First it's your watch, then your car, then your home, then what? Where does it stop?" He was determined to not let worries about what might happen keep him from enjoying what he loves. I certainly agree that you can't let others' animosity toward success keep you from enjoying being deservedly successful—but we must be vigilant when it comes to personal value preservation and security.

Anti-rich sentiments are just one more thing for the wealthy to worry about, on top of the typical geopolitical and economic risks, war, kidnapping, robbery, etc. But despite these horror stories I am telling you of cartel takeovers and watch robberies, it is not a lost cause. You don't have to lock up your diamonds and never drive your favorite car again. You can keep the lifestyle you have earned. You simply need to take precautions. People just like you are going through hell in places where the tide has already shifted, and those who have prepared for it will be fine. Those who haven't, won't.

Trapped by Red Tape

It's important to note that it's not just tragedy that can land you and your assets in a dangerous situation like the ones we have explored throughout this book. Let's suppose for a moment that most of your net worth was invested in gold mines in Africa or in gemstone mines in South America. Well, that can get really precarious, really quickly. What happens when a war breaks out in the country your mines are in? Now you can't access the mines, and your workforce is scared away or recruited into the armies. Or maybe there isn't a war, but politics get in the way—environmentalists shut you down, or laws pass that restrict the amount of mining or method of mining you can engage in, or a new president is elected who doesn't like you or your industry for whatever reason.

I had a client once who, years earlier before I knew him, wanted to move out of his eastern European home country and into a safer, more democratic and affluent country with his family, but the government of their country they were currently living in made that very difficult. In fact, they even ended up arresting this person on false charges, because the local government didn't want to lose the very substantial tax base that he and his businesses brought in each year. It was like he was a car manufacturer and the country was Detroit—but unlike Detroit, this country was *fighting* to keep him around, tooth and nail. Luckily for him, he had enough high-level supporters and thousands of employees who came together to ensure he was released, and after two years of incredible difficulties, he was able to move but was forced to leave a significant portion of his fortune behind. That was another situation where, like with the house taken over by the cartel, even if we had known him then, we simply would not be able to help. Too little, too late. I'll do a lot for my clients, but we don't fight entire countries' corrupt governing bodies for them.

I can't stress this enough: if you are of high net worth and own assets, businesses, and other forms of value around the world, this can happen to you. Look no further than the COVID-19 pandemic for proof. Did you expect, on December 31, 2019, to spend the next year locked inside your house? If I had gone back in time and told you on that day that you had better stock up on surgical masks and toilet paper, you would have looked at me like a conspiracy nut—but, well, those "unprecedented" times happened. For some, it affected their business very negatively. Millions lost their jobs and streams of revenue, on top of far too many people losing loved ones. If something like that happens again—or if another wave of COVID hits hard—travel restrictions could keep you from your assets. Maybe this happened to you—maybe you, like many of your clients, found yourself inextricably cut off from your vault in Europe, or unable to sell or rent your property because all the customers who may have been interested were trapped on the other side of the world.

Even forgoing those more dramatic—yet obviously, entirely possible—situations, there's stock market instability, hyperinflation (spurred by the broken fiat system), and an increase in regulations in many countries leading to many more complex challenges.

The question on many of my clients' minds is: where can I go? Is there still a safe haven somewhere? Well, the answer is that it is challenging everywhere. There are some safe havens, yes, but nowhere is completely without risk. Managing value is simply not as straightforward as it used to be. What one needs today, more than a specific location, is a truly diversified approach. A blend of fiat currency, physical assets and digital assets. Physical assets can provide a sense of stability for many, and fiat currency is still a necessary form of value for the time being—but the strategic addition of intelligently designed digital assets provides benefits that are not available via any other asset class. With digital forms of value, you have the potential to trade quickly without losing your valuable time and, in many cases, preserving great monetary value in the process as well.

Idoneus was created specifically for the purpose of value exchange and preservation. Carefully designed applications of this new technology can provide you with options, even when the rest of the world seems to be falling to pieces around you. Our clients have access to opportunities many others will not have when everything else seems dark. A candle in a blackout.

Even when you are not in danger, the ability to access and redeploy equity you hold or otherwise monetize your asset base at will is extremely important. Vital, even. You no longer need cash to acquire your next asset; you only need the ability to monetize what you currently have. As discussed, the concept and importance of value exchange is not new; it is a proven strategy, which is thousands of years old, with worldwide application. We have simply found a more efficient way to accomplish value exchange, and by now, I hope you are beginning to agree with me on the importance of this discovery.

Diversification is No Longer Enough; Mobility is Required

The more wealth you have, the more important it is that you have a system in place to move your wealth and value swiftly, safely, and legally. That's where we come in.

Because of our unique experience over the years, we have learned one key ingredient many others working in the high-value asset space often don't take as seriously as we do: discretion. Discretion is a fundamental key to each and every one of our relationships, with clients and with every trade partner we come in contact with. If you are escaping tyranny, if you are repositioning away from growing anti-wealth sentiments, if you are mobilizing to move out of a bad situation with the assets and people you care about most in a safe and quick manner, nothing is more important than the ability to do so quickly and without making any unnecessary waves. You can now move your asset base quickly and securely, without ever having your business being on public display.

As I've mentioned, my core operating principles are built on tenets of integrity, loyalty, and discretion, which I learned through hard-earned experience and which are more important than ever in these trying times. I believe our team at Idoneus will be able to help many families in Europe, the Caribbean, North, Central, and South America, in this way, in the very near future, as things begin to take a very challenging turn in many of these areas.

You must be able to operate within your *own* economy. You must not be tied to any single asset, currency, or locale. This requires independence, and in the world of value movement, it is now enabled by integration of blockchain technology into your strategy. We are a leader in this process and are delivering the solution for the future—available today.

You need a balanced approach to diversification—but I trust that you know this. If you're reading this book, you know how important it is to diversify both geographically and across asset classes, so I'm not going to waste your time explaining something you already know—and, if you're savvy, are already doing. What you *may not* know is that diversification is *not* enough. In today's day and age, you will need more than diversification. Today, mobility is also required.

If you are not highly mobile, when tragedy strikes, everything you worked so hard for is very likely going to disappear. Like smoke. It has happened to countless numbers of successful and experienced people before you, and today's climate means it could happen to you. Yes, you. Yes, no matter what your circumstances currently are.

Please don't put yourself and your family in danger out of fear of the future. Yes, the strategies utilizing blockchain, asset tokenization, and modern-day value-for-value exchange may be unfamiliar, but it is the future. Take the time to study these new opportunities, to learn about them, to understand them. It is easier than it seems at first blush, and I promise—one day, you'll look back and you will hardly be able to believe you went for so long without them.

In Summary

It can happen to anyone, and today's dangerous, increasingly unstable, anti-wealth world means it may happen sooner and to a greater degree than you think. You need to have a solution in place to protect your value before tragedy strikes, and Idoneus offers one such solution. If you ask me, it's one of the best solutions—though, I may have some bias there.

Once safety is established and their assets are what they want them to be, many of our clients still, however, don't feel completely satisfied. Why? Because "preserving value" goes beyond personal value. It refers to the value we all share as members of the human race, and of the population of the planet. If you have achieved safety and have made some solid strides that have led you to significant monetary success but still feel a hint of emptiness, you'll want to keep reading into the next chapter. It will be well worth your time.

Next, we will discuss opportunities and responsibilities when it comes to preserving the planet's value for coming generations—it's more rewarding than you have ever imagined!

Chapter Eight

Sustainability in a Rapidly Changing World

"The greatest wealth is the richness of soul."
—Muhammad

We've talked about that family a lot throughout this book—that family from the introduction that was airlifted out of their mansion; that family that, one day (though, hopefully not) could be your family. Well, let's go back, rewind time, and give that poor family a happier ending. I want you to imagine that that family did things a little differently, a little more strategically. Let's say they called me when they first decided to divest of that beautiful island property and immediately engaged with Idoneus to monetize their assets and lateralize their value to a preferred holding even before that turbulent time began. Let's say that the riot and the subsequent civil war did end up happening, but the family had already traded through IDON and into other assets they vastly preferred and instead of experiencing it firsthand they watched the riot on television, thousands of miles away, safe and secure. The ending is quite different then, isn't it? The children grew up securely, the parents grew older, and as the youngest children left for college, the husband and wife began thinking about their legacy and how narrowly they escaped financial devastation.

But they did indeed escape it!

If you're reading this book, I probably don't have to tell you about the importance of estate planning (though, if you don't already have a will and trusts in place, I'd suggest you close this book and get that sorted right now!). Part of why many of you are doing all that you do, after all, is to secure a safe and easier life for your family and children, and that is most of our first priorities.

However, once you're certain that your family, children, and loved ones are provided for, you may feel what many of my clients—and myself—feel: a drive to contribute on a deeper level, not just to our families but to the world.

Giving Back and Paying Forward

When talking about the value of giving back, we strive to be an example. We want to make an impact, and we want to make sure that impact is a lasting one.

My loving wife, Veturia, has been the director of philanthropy for our family for nearly a decade. Her efforts have allowed us to be a part of providing assistance for thousands of families in our own community and abroad, but that's far from the only philanthropic work she does. She is also the founder of Our Daily Bread Tampa Bay, a local Tampa Bay, Florida, charity that was designed to feed struggling families, veterans, and single moms.

My wife spent her childhood in Romania, where she experienced the challenges of living under a communist regime. The first 10 years of her life were influenced by exposure to the simplicity of human needs and the power of kindness. At a very young age, she and her family fled to Germany in the hopes of building a safer life there—by the kindness of a single family in Germany who took them in, she learned the significant impact one good deed can have on someone's life. Decades later, after moving to the U.S. and witnessing the amounts of wasted food everywhere on a daily basis, she made it her mission to turn it all around and help give back to those who need it most in her local community. That charity has since grown from its very humble beginnings of her picking up a trunk load of bread from a local bakery to a regional force for good, where, together with our local community partners, we are now able to provide approximately 100,000 pounds of quality food each week to as many as 1,500 local families and many other support organizations in need every month.

Giving back has been in our DNA since the beginning, but we're not even close to being done. Veturia and I have a lot of big dreams in this area, and my clients are often those who share these dreams. Just as in the beginning, when I had business leaders sharing their wisdom with me as I started in the business world, now we have global leaders in the world of philanthropy sharing their wisdom with us as to how best to make a difference in solving the most critical problems we face in society. I am thankful to the many generous clients who have shared their hearts and their journeys with us to help us shape our own vision for giving back.

Asset Trading for the Greater Good

Our next step is learning how to combine our strength in value exchange with our passion for helping the greater community. In other words, our goal is to find a way to move more value to help more people. And it's the next step for much of our clientele, especially as times change and/or they grow older and learn, as I have, that we don't need as much as we thought we did.

Our next major focus as a company is in moving (or exchanging) value to help our planet as a whole, not just in order to protect and preserve the assets of our clients. I'm talking about the protection and preservation of extraordinarily valuable assets like water, power, food, land, and many of our world's other valuable natural resources.

There is enough water, electricity, and food to serve the population, but they run on archaic systems. We seek to create better ways to move this value globally in a manner that allows much more flexibility in the holding and distribution of these resources.

While we have much work to do to set this in place, our ultimate mission is clearly defined. We see a future where every high-value transaction we are involved with could automatically set aside dedicated funds for sustainability. For example: $100 million pledged in IDON today could, through collaboration with our clients and corporate partners, bring a billion dollars in future value dedicated to our foundation and nature fund for future generations! Not only will this encourage many new clients to use our services, it will have a positive ripple effect on the rest of the planet. I can already imagine how impactful it will be to be able to tell our clients, "If you transact through our company, for your next superyacht acquisition or sale, $1 million in currency will be pledged to our nature fund in your name." This is achievable within the dynamics of the economy we are building. It will be a win for the client, a win for Idoneus, a win for Earth, and a win for humanity!

Protecting Value and Building Legacy

In the not-so-distant future, we know that the most valuable assets won't be massive mansions, flawless diamonds, hypercars, yachts, or even gold mines. It will be something much more natural. Something that used to be common, but is increasingly rare.

Virgin, undeveloped, beautiful . . . land.

I want to protect land. Land with lakes, with natural springs of water, with rivers. I want land set aside and protected that can be used to grow food—real, sustainable food out of real, sustainable soil. I want to buy and protect natural, valuable assets, such as the rainforests and coastal lands, so they themselves, and all nature they support, are here in the years to come for our grandchildren and great grandchildren to enjoy and benefit from.

The statistics are out there, and if your eyes have been opened, you have seen them. This is an incredibly important moment in history, and will only grow to be even more critical as time goes on. We have already seen a shift away from the material, but in the future, even the transient values of "travel" and "free time" will no longer be the core focus. The youngest generations—and even the generations yet to be born—will likely scoff at a luxury timepiece like the one left on the poolside table of my client's mansion, instead choosing to devote their resources to conservation, protection of human life, and a myriad of high-value areas of purpose.

It's going to be very interesting to see what is valuable 10 or 15 years from now and what is not, as personal values shift and as the world continues to change. All I can say for sure is that I believe the planet and the ability to enjoy a quality life on it, is worth protecting, and I and my team will be devoting quite a lot of our energy and resources toward doing exactly this.

It is possible to achieve a great thing for yourself and for the planet via sustainability—one just has to realize that "value" is not only personal. This is not just about charity for the whole world, but for your own legacy and future generations—do you really want another megayacht, or would you gain more personal value if you put that money into a second trust fund? Should you hustle for a fifth Ferrari, or will you find it more luxurious to take a month off to spend with your children, having experiences they will never forget? These are questions we all must answer and live with. To be clear, there is no judgment from me. I am one of the few that truly believes you can have it all!

Personally, I'm working on my own legacy right here, in these pages. Sure, I could have taken this time to make another trade, or gain another client, or inspect another physical asset, but instead, I decided to devote many hours and days of my life toward writing this book. I know how valuable the information in this book has been to me, and I hope it is not only valuable for you and countless other readers, but to my own children when they grow older and need guidance developing and securing their own forms of value in an ever-changing, complex world. The reflection required to write this book has been valuable to me as well, and I hope the information within it is transformational for everyone who reads it.

As one begins the journey of giving back, again, we have to start by finding out what our values are. This might be difficult. Perhaps you haven't even really thought about your own values in regard to contribution, always just doing what you thought was the next prescribed step. But if we want to follow Gandhi's example and "be the change we wish to see in the world," well, we have to decide what change we "wish to see."

Maybe you want to devote some time to a river cleanup, or some financial resources to a local food bank. Maybe you want to go a step further and purchase land for the sole purpose of preservation. Whatever your goal is, if you are able, begin to give back—start today. You won't regret it. Giving value is a precursor to receiving it!

Giving back isn't necessarily selfless, by the way—you can protect land that you also vacation at, for instance, or you might in the future choose to give funds to important charitable projects just by simply completing a transaction with our company, therefore adding more utility and value to the ecosystem, and in tandem, your own buying power. You could give to a foundation and secure your legacy via your name on an eco-friendly building designed to shelter the homeless, or build a theater for underprivileged children to find their voices and passions. If you have the ability to make a positive change and have not yet begun, what are you waiting for? Time waits for no one. If you will indulge me, I would like to share a bit of our vision for the future of philanthropy at Idoneus, but before I do, I want to take a moment here to thank the team at Goldpvnk for their countless hours invested with me and our team to help us crystalize our vision and execution plan for the next chapter in our journey, which is outlined in the following pages.

I and our entire team seek to make an impact with an organization we are launching called SOUL.

The Ultimate Luxury is Time

> *"Money has not made anyone happy yet. The more*
> *you have, the more you want. Instead of filling a*
> *vacuum, it makes one."*
> —*Benjamin Franklin*

SOUL is a nonprofit organization created by visionary team members at Idoneus. SOUL will make a measurable impact by allowing high-net-worth individuals to participate in an endeavor that allows them to leave a real legacy for future generations. From nature preservation, education, community parks and centers to environmental movements and circular economies, SOUL is the gateway that allows wealthy individuals, families, and organizations we work with to make an impact that withstands the test of time.

Content for Good

SOUL has an ambitious goal to create a new "content for good" platform, and the core focus will be to fund and mentor documentary films and television shows. SOUL will drive universal stories that need to be told to the masses via strategic alliances with major distribution channels. SOUL in partnership with world-class influencers, who collectively reach tens of millions of people across social media and are passionate and determined to make a lasting positive global change.

In addition to normal distribution channels, the influencers will allocate their reach and resources for positive change. The influencers will appear in films, working alongside our clients and team members and award-winning filmmakers producing much needed content for good.

The core of our content will cover many global issues, including endangered species, poaching, climate change, global fishery collapse, ocean pollution, homelessness, sex trafficking, gender equality, child mortality, hunger, resource migration, disease pandemics, nuclear security, cybersecurity, universal education, factory farming, biosecurity, and many other issues in need of the spotlight.

The top documentary filmmakers in the world spend around 80 percent of their time in search of funding and 20 percent of their time telling stories. SOUL is seeking to change that. We want storytellers to tell stories that will educate and entertain the world. We intend to link top global filmmakers together with influencers to create content that can change the world.

In a corrupt world of financing, where truth is hard to find, blockchain technology is again solving this issue by decentralizing global transactions and illuminating accountability. In the media world where once honorable news networks now simply feed ideologies, and more countries seem content to exist under a fluttering false flag, we at SOUL believe that filmmakers who are making "content for good" can decentralize media by funding independent, investigative journalistic films.

SOUL is also committed to creating a number of truly valuable philanthropic filming experiences that will connect our capital partners, who will follow the filmmakers and influencers around the globe as we travel with the world's top influencers, seeking solutions to our planet's greatest obstacles.

Once the films are finished, SOUL will distribute by pushing short video clips and film trailers to millions of global citizens, using their global reach to change the world, while illuminating the importance of content for good. Our films will have a powerful launch into television, digital streaming, education, and interfaith global distribution by using brand integration and social media channels. In addition, SOUL will support the film and media campaigns for red-carpet events, film festivals, and world premieres.

The films will be used as a tool to raise millions of dollars for the most efficient and effectively run not-for-profit organizations in the world, to support the illumination of global issues. Our vision is that SOUL will become a beacon of light, hope, and change for good. The world will come to know all about SOUL via the continuous campaign of press and media releases we have planned to support our endeavors.

*As humans, we are drawn to beauty. As humans with a
conscience, we are drawn to capturing impactful actions with
the hopes of making the world a better place.*

Our influencer partners have a social media audience
into the millions. SOUL's documentary series will use this
incredible resource to its full potential, creating real positive
change, highlighting the beauty, pain, and courageous people
fighting for change.

Combining documentary, high-end photoshoots, and
short, highly shareable digital content, our goal is to create a
beautiful and inspiring series that creates maximum reach and
maximum impact.

Our influencers will work on the ground with associated
nonprofit organizations while on location filming. From the
income generated from brand sponsors, and support from
Idoneus and our valued clients, SOUL will make donations
to these nonprofit organizations during the filming of each
episode. One hundred percent of the net proceeds raised
through donations garnered from each film will also be donated
by SOUL and the influencers to the respective nonprofit
organizations.

The influencers will tell the following stories through
narrative exposition, real-life events that combine actuality with
explanation and commentary. We'll also conduct interviews
with key personnel, along with reenactments where necessary,
and use archival footage to show historical events.

Conservation and Preservation in the Paradise of Costa Rica

Idoneus is building the new economy of luxury asset exchange and investing in the most valuable asset of all: nature. Through its reputation and track record in the global luxury/high-value marketplace, Idoneus is already promoting healthy assets and sustainable development in Costa Rica to set itself as an example to the world. Idoneus plans to create disruptive real estate development partnerships that promote conservation and preservation around the world.

Green Assets for Conservation: When did we stop believing that we are part of something bigger than ourselves? There is a language that we do not see but unites us in an invisible space. It is the language of nature, and it is through it that we recognize our true connection. Connecting with the plants and the trees, with the waters of the rivers and oceans, with ourselves, our neighbors, our children, and with the security that gives us, reminds us that we are an important part of a whole.

Wild Nature, One of Humanity's Most Valuable Assets

Our connection with nature is deep within all of us, and it brings us together to live our best life. Imagine a pristine rainforest and crystal-clear waters of the Caribbean lapping its shores. Imagine being part of a conservation legacy project that provides fulfillment for you and your generations to come. Imagine the ability to experience co-ownership of a luxury tropical jungle lodge where tokenized carbon credits are generated as value for investors. With participation in this investment via the Swiss payment token (IDON), a secure digital currency that provides peace of mind in today's volatile financial environment. How do you want to make your contribution? The choices are almost endless.

ENDANGERED SPECIES - AFRICA: Some of the world's most beloved animals are going extinct. Kenya is known for its safaris and national parks. With elephants facing so many threats, it's no surprise we find them on the endangered-species list. Some of the main struggles they face are poaching, loss of habitation, and lack of water. Big cats that you hope to see on these safaris are either on the threatened or endangered list. Because of the rise in temperatures, cheetahs are having a hard time reproducing, extreme droughts are bringing tick-borne diseases to lions, and big cats overall are facing a world of new problems. Giraffe numbers are dwindling across Africa because of poaching and habitat loss caused by human population growth, according to wildlife experts, and it's happening largely unnoticed. As humans come into contact with chimpanzees more readily through bushmeat availability and open-access logging roads, the spread of zoonotic diseases such as Ebola, a deadly hemorrhagic fever, threaten both human and ape populations.

OUR OCEANS: So much life begins in our oceans, and it remains today fundamental to our existence. The ocean's awe-inspiring power and abundance often overshadows its equally fragile nature. Our oceans are in trouble, and without immediate action, we are in real danger of losing the underwater world that sustains life on Earth forever. It is being reported that in the past 50 years we have lost 90 percent of the ocean's fish and nearly half of our coral reefs have disappeared. Even now, it is not too late. If we are vigilant, if we all become ambassadors for change, we can restore our wild and magnificent oceans, as we are the caretakers of the planet, and in order to have a healthy planet, we need healthy oceans.

ANIMALS AS ENTERTAINMENT - THAILAND: Animals in the entertainment world live a life of torture and deprivation. They are often kept in cages too small for them and are forced to work long hours without food, water, or rest. These animals are separated from their families at young ages and killed when they become sick or too old to perform.

MELTING ICE CAPS - THE HIGH ARCTIC: Everyone is well aware of the relationship between global warming and the rising sea levels. With Alaska's glaciers rapidly melting, it creates a substantial problem for both humans and animals. Scientists from the University of Alaska have calculated that the state will receive roughly a foot of water every seven years due to the melting glaciers. With less ice and more water, animals such as polar bears are drowning in the search of finding resting points. The rising water means flooding in coastal communities and more severe storms.

DEFORESTATION - BRAZIL: Rainforests play a huge role in helping stabilize the Earth's climate. The problem is as we emit higher carbon levels we're also deforesting the rainforest, making it impossible for these dense jungles to keep up with regulating climate. Brazil is home to the largest area of the Amazon Rainforest, which houses 10 percent of species known to the world. The good news is there are people fighting to protect this magical place. But even if we can save it from deforestation, it still faces droughts and other threats. Seventy percent of the Earth's land is used to produce grain primarily to feed the animals we eat. Deforestation is indeed the primary threat to the orangutan, a species of great ape known for its keen intelligence and the fact that it's the largest animal to live primarily in trees. The result has been the loss of some 80 percent of the orangutan habitat in just the last two decades.

DOMESTIC ANIMAL WELFARE ABUSE - USA: In the last 20 years, researchers and advocates have learned a lot about how pet abuse and domestic violence are related, and how important this relationship is for early identification of both human and animal victims of abuse. Over time, some information may have become distorted or oversimplified. Multiple studies have found that 49 to 71 percent of battered women reported that their pets had been threatened, harmed, and/or killed by their partners. In a national survey, 85 percent of domestic violence shelters indicated that women coming to their facilities told of incidents of pet abuse.

GLOBAL WARMING EFFECTS ON FOOD PRODUCTION - INDIA: With India having such a large coastal line, it is a country more vulnerable to global warming. They have already experienced devastating floods in their crop fields as well as severe droughts. The countries who will experience the tragedies of global warming the most are the poorer countries. The countries who can't afford to lose crops or homes, and who can't withstand the rising heat. The countries like vibrant India.

HUMAN TRAFFICKING - USA: An estimated 600,000 to 800,000 people are trafficked throughout the world every year. Many sex-trafficking victims are brought into the industry between the ages of 12 and 14 years old, and there are an estimated 20 million slaves in the world today. This is a global issue happening all over the world, even in the United States of America.

THE IVORY TRADE - CHINA: The demand for ivory to make decorative items, jewelry, and trinkets is pushing elephants to the brink of extinction. Burgeoning demand fuels poaching and trafficking, both of which are as dangerous as global arms, human, and drug trafficking. In addition to supporting anti-poaching measures, Earth Angels Destination Change will address all the links in the ivory chain, from source to transit to consumption.

HOMELESSNESS - USA: There are many different reasons for why people become homeless, such as escaping abuse, veterans with disabilities from war, mental illness, etc. The government hasn't come up with a good plan to end homelessness in America, but there are people who have. It is inexcusable for a country so rich to go to sleep with children and military veterans on the street.

These are just a few of the areas that we intend to bring attention to in our efforts to improve the world and help to preserve its value. If you feel like there is something missing in your life, perhaps you will consider putting your heart and mind to work in one of these areas with us. I and the world will thank you if you do. And if you're not sure how to do so, well, by this point you know exactly who to call to help you.

In Summary

Preserving value is just as important as creating it. If we can't preserve it, we will never be able to pass it on for future generations.

After you and your own value are secured, consider using a portion of that value to give back to the greater human community and beyond. Let me encourage you to write down what you value as I have above—be that the local community, animal life, children, nature, and so on—and then make decisions to take action to protect what you value. Consider joining us in the vision we have with SOUL. We would be honored to have you with us.

Value is changing, and we need to change with it. We are not doing this for accolades or to look good in the eyes of others, but out of a sincere concern for our planet and the life living on its surface. We are doing this for our and your safety, for those of us here now and for those generations coming in the future. If you are not already actively engaged in this effort (and I know many of you are), I sincerely hope you look within yourself and find it in your heart to give back however you are able. You might be surprised to find just how much of you wishes to involve yourself in the well-being of others, and just how much you will be willing to do to secure the safety of them and all others on this planet.

CONCLUSION

By now, you can look back at that family airlifted from the roof of their mansion and see exactly where they went wrong. They thought such an event could never happen to them. They waited for the perfect buyer, they didn't engage a capable professional, and worse still, after years with no progress they sat and waited further, assuming they were safe. They lost a devastatingly large portion of their fortune in a single day, relying on a false sense of security.

You now know how to avoid such an outcome.

You now know the importance of not only acquiring assets strategically, but digitizing a portion of your assets; of not only achieving diversification, but mobility; of not only securing value for yourself, but for your children and hopefully for the rest of the planet. You now also know a bit of my story, and the story of how we arrived where we are today with Idoneus on the global stage. You also are beginning to understand the power of blockchain technology and, specifically, IDON when it comes to securing and moving value for individuals personally and even the world collectively.

You're in a much stronger position than you were at the beginning of the book—I trust we can both agree on that!

Before we go, I have a few last-minute pieces of advice to share with you. First, to wrap up our time together, and crystalize a few points, here are my Top Five Tips for Successful Value Exchange:

1. Know *what* you value and *why* you value it—before going into any transaction.
2. Create a measurable plan of action and begin moving toward your goal the very moment you have made a decision that something must be done. Do not delay!
3. Conduct thorough due diligence on the parties you are transacting with or, better yet, have a professional firm do it for you.
4. Make a *commitment* to completing the task in a timely manner no matter what challenges you come up against.
5. Never ignore your instincts along the journey. When the road is filled with distractions, high cliffs, twists and turns, if you listen to that quiet voice within you, your internal compass will guide you to safety and security every time.

If you enjoyed this book and would like to learn more about what we are doing in the field of value-for-value exchange, please visit www.idoneus.io to stay updated on our progress.

Truly, thank you for reading this book—not just for me, but for you and for those who count on you, or will count on you in the future. It is one of my missions to share with the world the critical importance of understanding value, not only from a traditional perspective but from a historic viewpoint, as well as where and how value will be derived and monetized in the future. It is my belief that in the process we can make the world a better place, a safer place. A world with more options and more security for everyone and every living thing.

Together, we can begin to define and exchange value in new ways. Together, we can improve the way things are done, taking advantage of new technology to step into a future without borders and without limits. Together, we can create a new economy of trade—and a new world of opportunities—for ourselves and future generations.

ACKNOWLEDGEMENTS

This book would not have been possible without the impactful influence of many incredible people who have invested in me along the way. Thank you to those who took the time to teach me the lessons and values as a youth, which I still operate with today. To Mr. Edwards, who gave me my first job at the age of 9. Thank you for teaching me the importance of finishing work and the pride that comes from a job well done. To Mr. Doster, who hired me at the age of 13 and gave me an opportunity in a business before anyone else would. Thank you. To Lt. Col. Andreson, USMC, who saw my potential at age 15 and gave his recommendation on my behalf to the Marine Military Academy. To Sgt. Maj. Brown, USMC, your example of leadership and excellence has never been forgotten!

To my valued clients and associates, many who have become dear friends and trusted advisors, thank you from the bottom of my heart. Special thanks to Paul, James, Richard, Robert, Nikki, Ron and so many others. I will always be grateful for your wisdom, support, and faith in me. To the entire team at Idoneus, thank you for your tireless commitment to revolutionizing the industry that I love so much, and thank you for allowing me the opportunity to lead our organization through such an exciting time in the company's history. Each of you have my respect and sincere admiration. A special word of acknowledgment must be given to my dear friend and business associate of many years. Tim, what a journey! Thank you for taking it with me. Thank you for your relentless pursuit of excellence for our clients and for your continued efforts to become the best version of yourself, which adds value for everyone you come in contact with.

Thank you to Sixto and Susan for the love and light you share with our family and so many others. Your wisdom, prayers, and support have been an extraordinary gift.

Lastly, to my loving wife Veturia-Elena, thank you for your care, encouragement, and love. Each of my days are happier than the last because of the love you so generously give to me and our family. It is my honor and privilege to be your husband and partner in this life.

ABOUT THE AUTHOR

Raised humbly in a small town among the beautiful backdrop of nature in the Pacific Northwest region of the United States, Jarrett Preston's foundational focus on value was carved from a challenging childhood and during his time at the Marine Military Academy, Virginia Military Institute, and through his service in the United States Marine Corps. At the age of 21, he took his values of trust, integrity, courage, and commitment into the world of business. From the ground up, with an innate understanding of how physical assets could be traded and valued in new ways to increase wealth and diversify risk, he progressed rapidly, with a few bruises and many valuable learning moments along the way. In the world of luxury trading, he created Obsidian International Asset Trading with talented colleagues and grew it to become a multibillion-dollar portfolio and global client base.

Now the Chief Executive Officer of Idoneus, a Swiss blockchain-based asset trading platform and digital economy, he is dedicated to providing trusted service to HNW and UHNW clients and partners, increasing the value of the global luxury asset sector as we move into the modern era of finance.

Jarrett is also a family man, both husband and father, with the strongest of personal values and faith with a mission to make a lasting contribution to the world that goes beyond his business enterprises as a philanthropist.

www.ingramcontent.com/pod-product-compliance
Lightning Source LLC
Chambersburg PA
CBHW051825150726
47998CB00001B/298